SIGNS OF THE KINGDOM IN THE SECULAR CITY

SIGNS OF THE KINGDOM IN THE SECULAR CITY

COMPILED BY
DAVID J. FRENCHAK AND CLINTON E. STOCKWELL
EDITED BY HELEN UJVAROSY

COVENANT PRESS
Chicago, Illinois

ISBN 0-910452-56-3
Copyright © 1984 by Covenant Press
Cover art and design by David R. Westerfield
Production assistants: Jane K. Swanson, Naomi Wood, and Elsa Wiberg

COVENANT PRESS
3200 West Foster Avenue, Chicago, Illinois 60625
(800) 621-1290, (312) 478-4676

CONTENTS

PREFACE

Most of the articles in this compilation were originally presented at the 1980 SCUPE Congress on Urban Ministry, "Resources for the Urban Church." A major theme that emerged from the conference was the relationship of the kingdom of God to the city. The substance of this collection builds on that theme.

Section One, "The City," focuses on the nature of the city and the facts of global urbanization. In "To Build a City," Stanley Hallett, faculty of the Center for Urban Affairs, Northwestern University, and adjunct faculty with SCUPE, discusses the ecology of the modern city. Hallett challenges the modern assumptions that bigger is better and that increased technology necessarily leads to a greater sense of urban community. As a churchman, Hallett believes that the church's role in providing hope and offering experiences of community are vital to the building of viable urban neighborhoods.

"The Field Is the World and the World Is Increasingly Urban," by Samuel Wilson, first appeared in *The Standard* (February, 1981). Wilson, associate director for Missions Advanced Research and Communications (MARC), World Vision International, introduces his readers to some startling facts and statistics about worldwide urbanization. He urges church leaders to give urban training top priority in their stategic planning for global missions. According to Wilson, 264 cities in the developing or Third World nations will have populations of one million or more by the year 2000. With the developed world also already more than 70 percent urban, Wilson believes that any relevant missions strategies must be increasingly directed towards the growing needs of urban peoples.

Section Two, "The Kingdom," focuses on the nature of the kingdom of God and its symbolic and practical importance for urban mission. In "Signs of the Kingdom," George Webber, president emeritus of New York Theological Seminary, analyzes some classical misrepresentations of the kingdom. Arguing for a renewed understanding, Webber offers a new definition of the kingdom as a community of growth, nurture, and servanthood. Webber sees Christians as living signs of the kingdom, called to demonstrate unity, maturity, and servanthood in a world of need.

Tom Sine, researcher and planner for World Concern, offers another biblical perspective on the kingdom of God in "The Future—on Earth as It Is in Heaven." Sine, author of *The Mustard Seed Conspiracy* (Word, 1982), notes that North American intellectuals and clergy often share negative images of the city. He suggests that a biblical model of the future is necessary if we are to face the future with hope. For Sine, a key sign of the kingdom of God is mission to the city and to the urban poor. However, he also suggests that the biblical vision of the future is the urban image of the New Jerusalem found in Revelation. Because God's future is urban, Sine argues, the church needs to be more involved in the city today.

Section Three, "Theological Perspectives," offers two different theological perspectives on urban mission. Richard J. Mouw's "A Reformed Theological Perspective on Politics" attempts to define a Reformed theology of political involvement in the city. Mouw, a professor of philosophy at Calvin College, uses the biblical image of the New Jerusalem to encourage Christians to work for political justice now even as they await that "city whose builder and maker is God."

Dwight J. McFadden, Jr., former member of the Mennonite Church General Board, writes as an Anabaptist. In "An Anabaptist Theological Perspective on Economic Growth," he isolates five key themes from the Mennonite Confession of Faith: God's creation and providence, the nature and mission of the church, discipleship and nonconformity, and love and nonresistance, and relates them to urban ministry and social concerns.

According to McFadden, Anabaptists approach economic development as a communal activity, based on sharing and compassion, not accumulation and exploitation. As he sees it, the mission of the church in the city is to demonstrate that the kingdom of God and the church are a single entity in the world. His Anabaptist economic model underscores the importance of grassroots organizations as opposed to larger transnational commercial systems.

Section Four, "Evangelization and Renewal," examines evangelization and renewal among three ethnic communities. In "An Awakening Giant: Hispanics in the U.S.," Dr. Orlando Costas argues that Hispanics in the U.S. enjoy a rich religious and cultural heritage that has been basically ignored by North American evangelicals. Costas points out the great potential for leadership and mission within the Hispanic community. He cautions the white church that it is a grave error to ignore Hispanics in planning strategies for urban evangelization, and further warns that such strategies must be developed by and with Hispanic evangelicals, not for them. He points out how attitudes of white paternalism and homogeneous church growth have undermined the urban Hispanic American church. Costas ends by describing unique cultural patterns within the Hispanic community that tend to favor or discourage the spread of the Gospel among Hispanics. Dr. Costas is on the faculty of Eastern Baptist Theological Seminary.

In "A Case Study in Black Church Renewal," the Rev. Jeremiah Wright, Chicago pastor and SCUPE adjunct faculty, describes renewal and growth at Trinity United Church of Christ in Chicago. For this church that is "unashamedly black and unapologetically Christian," Wright identifies two key themes in its renewal as a black church: Bible teaching and preaching, and an in-depth understanding and love of black history, music, culture, and people. Wright asserts that the black church in North America has much to be proud of today, and much to draw on from its own unique history and cultural heritage.

Finally, professor Wi Jo Kang, Wartburg Theological Seminary, recounts the struggle of Asian Americans in "The Background of the U.S. Immigration Policy Toward Asians: Implications for the Urban Church Today." Kang documents the discriminatory naturalization and immigration policies enacted against Asian Americans since the 1850s. Kang suggests that those who desire to work among Asian Americans first acquaint themselves with the history of Asian American relations. Kang also believes that urban missionaries must take the initiative to become familiar with Asian cultures and religious traditions if they are to reach this growing segment of urban society. Like Costas, Kang views the Asian community in U.S. cities as potentially open and receptive to Christianity. However, he cautions that Christian involvement in Asian communities must reflect a genuine sensitivity to the identity, heritage, and needs of Asian Americans.

Section Five, "Strategies of Ministry and Evangelization for the Urban Church," looks at methods and philosophies of urban ministry. Philip Amerson, director of Patchwork Central Ministries, Evansville, Indiana, and SCUPE adjunct faculty, gives readers a paradigm for Christian response and leadership in urban communities. "Ministry on the Urban Frontier: Access and Retirement," presents a theological rationale for a cooperative, nonpaternalistic model of urban ministry based on the story of the Gerasene Demoniac.

For Amerson, the purpose of urban ministry is to establish contact with the poor and to encourage them to seek and meet their own needs. While some urban mission strategies for the poor foster dependency on the mission or missionary, Amerson prefers a model that empowers the poor by connecting them to needed resources and encouraging them to make their own decisions. Once contact and identification with the poor have been achieved, Amerson favors voluntary retirement in order to allow new leadership to emerge. Amerson sees a similar pattern of access and retirement in the incarnation and ministry of Jesus that allowed his disciples to develop and experience the power of their own faith.

The final article is perhaps the most concrete. Clinton Stockwell's "Barriers and Bridges to Active Christian Presence in Urban Neighborhoods," gives practical suggestions on how individual pastors can identify needs, resources, and strategies in their own urban parishes. According to Stockwell, evangelization can best be defined as an ongoing wholistic process that grows out of active Christian presence in urban communities. Stockwell points out barriers to this process and offers suggestions for developing urban evangelization strategies based on meaningful Christian presence. Clinton Stockwell is director of SCUPE's Urban Church Resource Center.

The compilers wish to thank all those who contributed to this collection. Special thanks are given to Rosalie Dvirnak and Priscialla Eisaman for typing the drafts.

Also, thanks to Professors Orlando Costas and Wi Jo Kang for their original contributions. Finally, the compilers wish to thank Helen Ujvarosy for her careful and thorough editing of the text and for her efforts to communicate a wide range of theological concepts to the diverse readership intended for this volume.

THE CITY

TO BUILD A CITY

Stanley J. Hallett, professor, Northwestern University

City watching these days is like looking into a kaleidoscope that is beginning to spin, the colors blurring. Too much is changing too fast, and we experience the vertigo that comes from not knowing how and where to fix our eyes and balance our inner ears.

It is important to understand why these changes are taking place. Our situation is analogous to the investigations into the earth's structure in the early 1950s. The Oceanographic Institute outfitted a ship with sonar to take soundings of the ocean depths. The ship discovered that the ocean is not a big bathtub. Instead, there are huge expanses that are flatter than the Salt Flats of Utah, crevices deeper than the Grand Canyon, and mountains that rise higher than the Himalayas, all buried underneath the surface of the ocean.

During this same period, studies were going on of volcanoes, earthquakes, and the geological structures of the continental shelves. In 1956, scientists from the Institute suggested to a scientific conference that all of this information would make sense if there were floating plates that formed the structure of the earth's crust. The motion of these plates, they suggested, opened up the crevices and threw up the mountains. According to this view, Mount St. Helens burped as a result of the pressure building from the Pacific plate moving in under the Continental plate.

When first introduced, the notion of plate tectonics was laughed at because people did not want to deal with the idea that the ground underneath their feet was shifting. But the theory makes some sense out of what seemed like a whole range of disparate information.

Cities could use a comparable theory about fundamental shifts in their basic structures. In the past, three groups of structural assumptions combined to shape the modern industrial city.

The first set of assumptions dealt with growth. It was widely believed that population growth would continue to show steady gains in urban areas; that resources would be cheap, available, and unlimited; and that the environment could withstand anything anyone wanted to throw into it.

A second set of assumptions dealt with economic growth and with government services. The feeling seemed to be that the mere production of

3

wealth would release humankind from its slavery to necessity; that the development of technology would meet all needs; that technology should be labor-saving, capital- and energy-intensive, and centrally controlled; that the primary instrument for technological development was the modern corporation; and that any problems left over after business had produced enough could be solved by increasingly professionalized and bureaucratized social services, including more hospitals, schools, and police.

The final set of assumptions dealt with government. These maintained that government should provide the framework within which people could pursue their own interests; that the government basically should be an impartial referee, but should also supply the money for the installation of the infrastructure (roads, water, sewers, and research and human capital development); that it should pay for the development of a trained, educated work force; that it should provide minimum access to necessary goods and services (welfare, Medicaid, food stamps, unemployment, Social Security); and that apart from these tasks the role of government should be strictly limited.

These three sets of assumptions imply that more is marvelous and that centralization is the primary goal for social organization, technology, and services.

Given these implications, religion itself becomes a residual category because if the social order is working well, then the primary task of the church is the care and cure of souls, or patching people up in order to throw them back into the social order. As a result, religion tends to be increasingly concerned with the private sphere of family and leisure time rather than with questions of vocation and meaning. Furthermore, if centralization is truly optimal, then local phenomena are meaningless and marginal by definition. That makes the neighborhood a marginal category, and the community church merely a residual institution attached to a local appendage of a large-scale, centrally organized system, which, thank you very much, is working quite well.

The trouble is that none of the assumptions hold. The population is not expanding. In the past decade Chicago, for one, has had a net loss of more than 600,000 people. The ideas that it is up to the government to reward growth through a series of tax incentives, and that the government should make investments of public capital to transform cornfields into suburbs are also highly questionable.

In addition, the economy is now facing serious problems because of declining resources, notably oil—and soil. Farmers lose eight to ten tons of topsoil per acre planted in corn in land that can withstand only two or three tons of loss. Current agricultural techniques strip vital ingredients from the soil and replace them with energy-intensive fossil-fuel based fertilizers, as if there were no limits to the natural capital of the earth.

Furthermore, a society that used to think it could simply throw things away has now discovered that there is no longer an "away." What is away for one person is in somebody else's way, or, in fact, may come back full circle. The environment is not only throwing back, it is throwing up.

Industry's ideal technological model used to be very much like an open pipe—an efficient, labor-saving device for sucking enormous resources in one end and spewing huge amounts of goods and waste out the other. In general, industry treated nature as a mine on the one end and a sink on the other. That definition of efficiency is no longer adequate.

As for centralized systems, Chicago has a combined sewer area for four million people. When it rains, storm drains and sewage drains overflow into the river. To solve this problem the city is building a tunnel 200 feet underground, 30 to 35 feet in diameter, big enough for three trains to pass without touching. The tunnel will channel waste to a reservoir and pump it into a treatment facility. It will take a nuclear power plant to provide enough energy to accomplish this task.

The treatment facility will take organic sewage and form a sludge which will then be mixed with industrial chemicals and toxins so that it cannot be used for anything. It will cost $138 per ton to ship the sludge downstate and put it in abandoned strip mines. People downstate are saying that they have already taken as much of that from Chicago as they want to.

The cost of this little dream was originally estimated at $1.5 billion, then $4 to 6 billion, and the latest report is $13 billion. At the $6 billion level the deep tunnel will cost $4,000 to $5,000 per dwelling unit. That is enough to build whole new neighborhoods. In addition, if the organic waste from this city were put into anaerobic digesters and converted into methane and organic fertilizer, it would be worth a 1977 price of $250 million. Chicagoans could be cooking with genuine people's gas and also providing all the fertilizer they need for the greenhouses they are going to build.

The costs of these centralized systems rise as resources get scarce. Often production is moved to remote facilities that require very little labor, and therefore the costs of city living rise while the potential for income is diminished. Society then reacts by developing a whole set of substitutes for work in the form of expanded social and medical care services. It is now known that a whole range of illnesses are associated with the loss of purpose that accompanies the absence of meaningful work. In its efforts to remedy these symptoms, the only thing society has succeeded in doing is creating another enormous industry. The largest medical complex in the world is located next to the Eisenhower Expressway in the poorest section of Chicago.

In lower-class neighborhoods medical problems are primarily the result of poverty: personal attacks, malnutrition, lung ailments related to pollution. There are numerous ways to invest in positive health action. These include creating healthy environments and workable communities, shifting the focus of government aid from remedial services to community-building action, and changing the orientation of relief programs from professional-client relations to mutual aid. Instead, communities continue to pour huge resources into the care and cure system.

Cities enlist more police to contain the frustrations of young people who grow up fearing there is no opportunity for work. Ninety-five percent of burglaries are committed by people between the ages of sixteen and twenty-five who live within a mile and a half of the place where the burglary occurs. The problem in the city becomes one of protecting ourselves from our own children.

According to school principals on Chicago's South Shore, "Seventy percent of the kids who were there in the fall aren't there in the spring, and another 70 percent have taken their place and you can't educate a moving stream." Yet school boards continue to pump money into the schools to solve the problem of shifting student populations caused by people who do not have enough money to pay the rent and who must run from the landlord regularly.

These problems are part of a housing-income-work-technology continuum that ultimately reflects our basic social values. But these problems also raise questions about the possibility of reshaping government structures and policies in order to reward investments that contribute to the city and inhibit those that destroy it. What are the things that build a city?

Preliminary studies conducted in Chicago neighborhoods to find out the cost of entitlements such as welfare, unemployment, Medicare, and Medicaid indicated that in South Shore alone entitlements might amount to as much as $20 million per year. When the final numbers come back from the computer, however, it turned out that it took $62 million a year to sustain a neighborhood of 80,000 people in the absence of work. Furthermore, these payments created few if any jobs for the community.

This system of income maintenance actually discourages investment and credit. To allow credit is to believe in the future; to invest is to use power and resources to shape that future.

The key questions today are, what new directions might technology take in our current cities, and how can cities make their neighborhoods work again? Some of the neighborhoods established in the 1920s are probably better adapted to the technology needed today than many of the communities built during the 1950s and 1960s—older city neighborhoods actually have an advantage. But change requires community action at the neighborhood level. Technology doesn't just put itself in place. It is fairly easy to centralize urban investment developments (i.e., using funds from Aetna Insurance Company to build Fox Valley East between Aurora and Naperville) because one is starting with cornfields, and cornfields don't vote. But to transform South Shore or Humboldt Park is to deal with people, and any lasting change has to grow out of their lives.

As the impetus for change shifts from centralized institutions to local neighborhoods, the local church may be the place where the neighborhood's imagination starts to take form, where the community starts to build. The church may be the place where people begin to ask fundamental questions, and to create new possibilities about how they are going to organize their lives.

It is not enough to make it possible for people to survive as neighborhoods come tumbling down around their ears. They will need credit and investment resources if they are to build their communities, and this process would cost much less than $62 million a year!

In 1977, for the first time in Illinois, the cost of Medicaid was more than 50 percent of the total welfare budget. By 1981, it was 61 percent of the total budget. That means that the poor get 39 percent of the welfare funds to cover food, clothing, shelter, and everything else; doctors and hospitals get

6

all the rest. The poor have become the narrow neck in the hourglass through which the tax dollars flow on their way to the middle class. One good poor neighborhood with lots of multiproblem families now probably can provide the economic base for at least three middle-class neighborhoods.

Transformation begins at the neighborhood level when people decide that the neighborhood *is* the promised land. Then it is possible to see dramatic new possibilities for a new era of invention based on new sets of assumptions.

All this will require new technologies and new tools. To some extent, in Chicago, this already is happening. The Center for Neighborhood Technology is a group of organizations like the Community Development Corporation and the Rehab Networks, working with older neighborhoods to develop new principles that bypass open pipe and waste disposal technology in favor of resource recovery.

An alternative schools network is setting up co-ops where people can work part of the day and study part of the day so that students can earn enough to support the institution. Some neighborhoods are exploring the possibilities of a mutual security insurance company. Instead of inflating the police force and paying exorbitant insurance rates, at least 70 percent of the people in a block join together to restore the physical and financial security of the community.

Loan committees are also a viable option for neighborhoods. The First National Bank downtown could not work seriously at a neighborhood level because the cost of obtaining credit information about a $70,000 loan to a private South Shore school would be prohibitive. But a loan committee in the neighborhood would know the school's board, would understand its problems, and would know which families the community might lose if children could not attend the school. This committee would have all the information it needed to make a credit judgment.

Experience shows that top-down authority tends to promote dependency, but that decentralized authority allows neighborhood people to begin to shape their own lives.

One example might be community energy authorities, where people together can make decisions about neighborhood energy policies. They may want to cut consumption 5 percent a year for five years. They may decide to bargain with Commonwealth Edison to make sure the utility won't overbuild and dump its costs on the neighborhood. They may want to recycle their waste instead of putting so much money into a $6 billion hole in the ground. It is the only thing that will guarantee that even if Chicago goes down the drain, there will be one big enough.

What happens when people are simply turned loose? West Town, just east of Humboldt Park, is some of the roughest gang land in Chicago. But a little housing rehab corporation has enlisted members of one of those gangs. As they all work together, questions of rival territory are disappearing.

If people are turned loose, they will build a city. If people are set free, they will build a church. If people have hope, they will find the strength to get up and do the things that need to be done.

THE FIELD IS THE WORLD AND THE WORLD IS INCREASINGLY URBAN

Samuel Wilson, associate director,
MARC, World Vision International

Our task is to present in grand brush strokes a picture of urbanization around the world, and then to interpret the church's response to this situation.

Before we begin, let us quickly review some key facts about world urbanization. If the facts are not news, they will at least provide context and emphasis.

WORLDWIDE URBANIZATION

The United States became urban in majority about 1920, and officially suburban in plurality in the 1970s. Although the U.S. is now 75 percent urban, many North Americans tend to think of the rest of the world as rural, even when this is emphatically not so. At the turn of the century, there were only eleven cities in the world with populations of more than one million. In 1971, Harbrin, Nagoya, Pyongyang, Ubon, and Katchatani all had populations of at least one-and-a-half million, yet these cities were hardly household names. It is projected that in 1985, there will be 273 cities with more than a million inhabitants. Before the end of the century, major population centers in the less developed nations will have twice as many urban dwellers as cities in the industrialized world.

Of the world's population of 4.6 billion, 1.7 billion are now defined as urban. Urbanization has become a global phenomenon.

At the beginning of the 1980s, nearly 40 percent of the world's peoples lived in urban centers; of these, 25 percent lived in cities of more than 100,000. While most people think of the United States and the developed world as urbanized, few are aware that:

• One-third of the people living in underdeveloped nations live in cities.

• Sixty-one percent of Latin Americans live in cities.

• Thirteen of the world's twenty-five most populous urban areas are in less developed countries.

• Japan has three cities of more than seven million people each.

• Only thirty nations and one region (East Africa) are less than 15 percent urbanized.

• Metropolitan Tokyo is equal to one half the population of Canada.

9

• The ten largest cities of India are the equivalent to one half the population of Great Britain.

In 1970, four world cities contained ten million people each. By 1985, there will be at least seventeen of these cities, and more than half of them (at least ten) will be in the developing world. The century began with only eleven cities of one million or more. Today, there are more than that in Asia alone. Latin America is far more urban than the rest of the world as a whole, and nearly as urban as the developed world.

The speed and the social conditions under which urbanization is now occurring in the Third World do not permit these cities to develop in the same way as cities in the industrialized world. Sanitation, water, transportation, jobs, and schooling are not keeping pace, and these conditions are setting the stage for poverty, unrest, and global social change.

Today it is doubtful that a Third World city of consequence can be found where even one-half of the population is urban born. In the coming decades most of this urban growth will continue to result from rural migration.

URBANIZATION AND ATTITUDES

Mindsets, attitudes, and actions towards the city do not exist in a vacuum. In *The Intellectual Versus the City,* Morton and Lucia White summarize the history of attitudes toward city life. According to the Whites, early modern European scholars extolled the rebirth of medieval cities as the fountain of all civilized culture, but urban life has not fared as well in more recent appraisals. The current fear and distrust of city life shared by most clergy and church leaders are also common to contemporary intellectuals in general. These feelings have honest roots both in history and life experiences. The growth of the bourgeoisie, and industrialization with its attendant horrors turned a whole era against the city.

Today most suburbanites tend to be vehemently anti-city. Yet, as the "I Love New York" bumper sticker campaign shows, the object of their scorn becomes a sudden convenience when they want to see a Broadway show.

The United States and most of the rest of the world are in a turmoil of ambivalence, torn between loving and hating the city. It is hardly any wonder that church congregations are confused and uncertain about urban ministry.

To understand the attitudes of white majority churches to city ministries, we need a little historical background.

Stage One: Flight from the Center. For a convenient starting point, we can begin near the end of World War II. Churches everywhere were holding mortgage-burning ceremonies. The new war-induced prosperity and the beginnings of a headlong plunge into a consumer economy were making the American dream of a home for each family come true—in the suburbs. The city neighborhoods vacated by these new suburbanites became transitional zones where incoming blacks were seen as a threat. The problems of urban transitional neighborhoods persist today, unsolved for succeeding waves of replacement populations. When it was more convenient to leave, when the puzzle became too tough to solve, the church fled the city and built new buildings for its suburban membership.

10

Stage Two: Tentative Return Rebuffed. A tentative evangelical conscience (stirred, perhaps, by the inconsistency of investing so much energy in overseas missions) began to prick the suburban church, but efforts at ministry to inner-city blacks were understandably rebuffed. The suburban church had no great sensitivity to deep human needs, and no readiness to commit itself to involved action. A distorted notion of the Gospel deceived the church into thinking that social awareness and social concern were paths to ecclesiastical degeneration, and any overt social action was seen as a loss of evangelistic virginity. Today it may be hard to imagine the reality and strength of this persuasion.

Social perceptions are real in effect if they are acted upon as reality. The church, in common with a majority of North Americans, chose to avoid the city because of exaggerated fears of urban problems that were themselves outgrowths of this point of view.

In many ways the social problems of the central city did outstrip the resources of the church, especially a church that thought of totally resolving the problems instead of ministering as a faithful servant. And when it was more convenient to leave, when the puzzle became too tough to solve, the church maintained and rationalized its flight from the city.

Stage Three: Identification of "External" Resources. Persistence and vision gradually led to change. Little by little a few heroic souls overcame conceptual barriers and discovered a growing network of external resources to which informed urban clergy could link needy people. Justice, wonder of wonders, was not foreign to good theology if a knowledge of resources was available. The church began to see that spiritual ministry was possible in conjunction with concern for social justice, and to adopt the mental freedom to live in the world.

THE PRESENT CHALLENGE

The church in the United States now faces two new challenges which promise to be just as demanding as those of the past. First, the church-at-large needs to become more involved in the social action initiated in stage two. Second, ministry in the central city must be ready to deal with the erratic shifts that occur as fiscal realities collide with government aid policies.

Most United States cities with populations of half a million or more receive fifty cents in federal funds to match every dollar in local revenue. Even so, ten of our forty-eight largest cities are in financial distress and may face eventual bankruptcy. Aid to the urban poor is now a serious drain on national resources and many government planners are looking for new models of the city.

Tampa, Orlando, Houston, Phoenix, and San Diego are all expected to grow by more than 30 percent in the 1980s. The current pace of Sun Belt urban growth may itself be a latter-day version of the earlier flight from inner-city realities.

The character of central cities may also change in the 1980s. A trend toward revitalization will put increasing pressure on the poor who may be displaced but not eradicated. The disparity between the poor and rich will be aggravated as cities take on new roles as leisure and entertainment centers.

Poverty and dependency, though not inherently urban conditions, are rampant in northeastern cities due to a process of selective migration. For the most part, the middle and upper classes are gone and many poor people are trapped. The result is that the barrier to ministry in the city is higher for those who are not already committed.

Sweeping increases in home prices and shortages in apartments are also reducing mobility in metropolitan areas. However, a more stable urban population can enhance a sense of community, especially as increasingly acute problems are shared.

CITY AND COMMUNITY

It has taken a long time to admit that feelings of community can exist in the city. One of the reasons the city was viewed as such a horrendous place was that it was thought to represent the total breakdown of human ties. Sociologists got carried away by their own rhetoric and reinforced this popular myth with facile theoretical descriptions of depersonalization. Desperate problems did exist, but even so, human ties remained.

The question of community solidarity is important to anyone with humanitarian or evangelistic concerns. Community solidarity is the best way both to impress the establishment and to threaten its power. If the poor do not organize or in some way gain representation as a visible bloc or power, they will remain effectively disenfranchised.

The church undermines its claim to universality when it fails to minister to and speak as advocate for the many diverse social groups that make up the unity of the city.

Community dynamics are also of interest to those concerned about evangelism because strategies and tactics for evangelism grow out of perceptions of community and class loyalties. Vocabulary and lifestyle affect what one hears and how one reacts.

The United States has much to learn about urban problems. The challenge to the church is to find its place in the city of the future.

THE CITIES AND MISSIONS

Some have questioned whether the urban church will pass through similar sequences overseas, and whether solutions can also be similar there. It is no longer possible to deny the dominance of the city in planning for the world future. There are still rural masses in the world today, but urban people are now and will increasingly become the key force to be reckoned with.

Migrants now account for as much as 76 percent of population increases in Third World cities. Because of this massive influx, developing nations will become 50 percent urban by the year 2000, and problems will be concentrated and multiplied as never before. These cities will compress into two to three decades the same amount of growth that was spread out over seven to eight decades in the industrial cities of developed nations.

At one time, the primary stimulus of urban growth was industry's insatiable demand for labor. As a result, the layouts of Western industrial cities were largely determined by natural transportation networks and by later needs for mass transportation.

Research on migration in developing countries that borrows from Western sociological studies is in for drastic revision because the social, political, and economic forces that fuel migration are very different from the technological and industrial forces that produced Western urbanization.

Without downplaying the poverty backwatered in our own central cities, a look at urban conditions around the globe may point out some of the horrors that are developing in Third World cities.

RAPID GROWTH AND POVERTY

By the end of the century, one billion more people will live in the cities of the world's poor countries. They will be seeking work, and meaningful work will not be available. With cheap labor abundant, manufacturers will not enhance productivity by introducing labor-saving devices, nor will the work force tolerate any threats to job stability. The unskilled labor market will contain unbelievable potential for competition and upheaval.

One key feature of village or agrarian life is self-sufficiency. Not so in urban life. Developing world cities are nothing short of terrifyingly vulnerable in their dependence on external food supplies. Looming in the future is the grim specter of a world food distribution system that bypasses local populations.

Backing off from their blanket bleak projections of ten years ago, experts now say that the probable source of greatest difficulty in the future lies with the food supply, and that the most acute facet of the problem is not production limits but maldistribution. In most Third World countries food production is not increasing in the same areas as population growth, so that cities are vulnerable both to food shortages and to transport and distribution imbalances.

The end of the decade will see one billion people malnourished, many in cities. How will they be fed, housed, and clothed? How will the Gospel of a well-fed clergy answer the needs of these hungry? What reception will it receive as increasingly less identification exists between the church and the poor? Many of the disparities between the developed and developing world are more acute and much more acutely experienced in urban settings. More than 50 percent of the housing needs in developing nations are found among the 30 percent who live in cities. Only about 1 percent of their children go to universities.

Many migrants settle in so-called marginal or squatter areas. The Crossroads of South Africa, the Pueblos Jovenes of Peru, the Villas Miserias of Argentina, the Favelas of Brazil—the very names are a litany of horrors to anyone familiar with them. Especially in their early stages these settlements are completely devoid of any of the amenities usually associated with even minimal standards of living. Sanitation is nonexistent. Potable water must be trucked in. Forget education.

These urban migrant areas are frequently the targets of misdirected social and political action from governments that would prefer to eliminate these sore points rather than to redress them. South Africa once brought in bulldozers against them, but most other governments have attempted at least superficial improvement. Despite these desperate conditions, the migrant stream is unlikely to abate appreciably in the next decade.

The shock is to discover that, as bad as these urban habitats are, they are better than the rural conditions abandoned by the migrants. Only one-tenth of all country dwellers have access to public water, while one-half of city dwellers do. Calcutta headed off seven million refugees from Bangladesh, north of the city, but was not able to block those refugees who gained entry from the countryside. In the past, refugee movements across national boundaries were somewhat disruptive, but generally refugees of rural origins sought out rural locations and established and supported themselves through their own farming. As education becomes increasingly available to the villages of the world, more refugees have at least a primary education. Data now show that these educated refugees are adding to the dependent migrant wave that threatens these cities. In the coming decade, refugees will continue to be a sizable portion of the urban influx, particularly in Africa where these trends are already well established.

Worldwide urbanization is today's dominant theme. The wealth of nations is dominated by cities. Social change seems to have been invented here. Social scientists wrestle to understand the questions of urban systems and their interactions in order to plan for the secular future. Social commentators are increasingly uneasy about the potential for social unrest in countless urban ghettos worldwide. While the fears themselves may be overrated, the pathos of these millions of urban poor would wring from the Galilean a cry of anguished prayer.

MISSION AND THE OVERSEAS CITY

The first clear biblical instance of individual cross-cultural ministry was Jonah's direct call from God *to a major city*—Nineveh! Fifty percent of the world's projected population of 6.2 billion in A.D. 2000 will be living in cities. This number is more than the three billion now thought to be unreached by the Gospel.

In assessing the future of overseas missions, let us once again adopt a semihistorical approach. In the less urbanized world of the nineteenth century, mission boards (largely by force of circumstance) allocated a reasonable quota of their resources to foreign cities. These cities were colonial centers and business had to be transacted with the governments there.

There can be no doubt that Christian conscience provided the impetus for these first efforts overseas, even (or perhaps especially) in areas short of resources. Christian commitment has definitely had its place. One estimate claims that 18 percent of medical work in India is carried on by the 2.6 percent of the population reported as Christian. It is also true that the sweeping urbanization of the developing world is a fairly recent phenomenon. The population of Lima, Peru, for example, only slightly more than 500,000 in 1940, now exceeds five million.

However, by the time United States suburban churches were markedly increasing their support for overseas ministries, the public relations appeal of foreign missionaries as heroic and exotic was already well established. Many mission agencies capitalized on this image by concentrating on missions involving physical hardship and geographic inaccessibility. As a result, these missions tended to be rural, and also educational, since literacy was uncritically accepted as a veritable prerequisite of the Gospel. How often did missionaries lament that potential leaders were skimmed off for government jobs and lost to the church? It took mission boards quite a while to recognize that their converts had gone to major cities and were lost because the particular churches to which they belonged were virtually nonexistent in these power centers.

The next wave of urbanization transported adherents from rural churches to the city for other reasons. Ambivalence characterized this whole period. Older denominational missions with established city traditions reduced their commitment of personnel and other resources to their affiliated urban churches. National leaders in these churches were left with no resources to apply to swelling social needs. Newer missionary agencies tended to reflect the apolitical, asocial mindset of evangelical suburbia.

In the postindustrial era, the church in the United States learned to seek and match available resources to human need. The decade of the 1970s marked the arrival of evangelicals with the ability to raise domestic resources and to find matching international funds to minister to massive need. The Sahel Desert drought and the plight of Southeast Asian refugees both left indelible marks on U.S. missions thought and action.

Nevertheless, worldwide inflation is undermining these massive missions programs. Traditional forms of aid and church planting are increasingly too expensive for traditional fund-raising techniques. Furthermore, even as affluent suburban churches (who once shied away from social involvement at home) now quietly turn to missions activities overseas, poverty surges over the globe at an unparalleled rate. It is broadcast over the countryside; it multiplies and festers in every city in the world.

The problem of resources is serious indeed. Certainly, developing nations cannot offer resources they do not have. The telling question is whether the church (once fearful in the face of comparatively microscopic need) will now begin to live up to the Master's mandate, or whether it will once again flee the world's cities.

The scale of the problem can no longer be ignored. However, the first step in solving the problem is to ask the right questions, not to give the right answers. Mere funding has certainly not proved adequate.

As the church attempts to raise and answer appropriate questions, it might start with the following:

Who needs to be reached? The commission to go into all the world includes ministry to the cities of the world. The unreached are increasingly urban.

What are the most pressing needs? Unreached urban peoples increasingly live under conditions of subhuman poverty, massive unemployment, and life-threatening malnutrition.

Who should do the ministering? The entire church of Christ has an inescapable mandate to declare and to live the message of his love.

In the face of world need, it is crucial that the church begin to prepare missions candidates for city ministries. Church leaders might begin by asking themselves if they know the right questions to pose to national urban church leaders in Third World countries to help them develop their own innovative ministry programs. It is quite clear that set solutions will no longer work.

15

By the year 2000, there will be 264 cities in the developing world with populations of a million or more. If the history of urban mission in the United States is characterized by ambivalence and approach/avoidance tensions, the attitudes and commitments of international mission agencies constantly undergo similar swings.

One of the travesties of United States Christendom is its failure to call racial and ethnic urban churches to a vision of world need and to involvement in world mission. Black, Hispanic, and Asian inner-city churches all have important and unique insights and experiences to add to the worldwide evangelistic resources of the church at large.

Two New Testament Scriptures contain ominous overtones for the city. First, the triumphal entry of Jesus into Jerusalem was preceded by his grief and condemnation for the city of Jerusalem (Luke 19:41-44). Second, the hope of his second coming is saddened by a similar note of grief: "You will not have gone through all the towns of Israel, before the Son of man comes" (Matthew 10:23). These warnings underscore both the urgency and the seriousness of urban mission as a task for the people of God.

THE KINGDOM

SIGNS OF THE KINGDOM LUKE 7:18-23

George W. Webber, president emeritus,
New York Theological Seminary

INTRODUCTION

The kingdom of God is a major theme of biblical faith throughout both the Old and the New Testaments. The importance of the kingdom was a favorite topic in the church where I grew up. The pastor, a proponent of the liberal social gospel and a man of great Christian faithfulness and maturity, used to preach that Jesus taught just one thing: "The supreme importance of human personality." He continually reminded us that every person was a child of God, and that God had made of one blood all those who dwelt on the face of the earth. At the same time, his prayers had one consistent note: "Help us, O God, to bring in thy kingdom." To a boy sitting in that congregation, our calling seemed unequivocal. Christians were to do everything in their power to bring in the kingdom. If they were faithful, they could expect to see the last of racism, war, poverty, and injustice.

What a shock then to arrive at Union Theological Seminary in 1946 and discover almost overnight that such social gospel optimism was thoroughly out of style. To the new generation, the Great Depression and the shattering experience of World War II seemed evidence enough that the earthly kingdom of God was nowhere near at hand. Everywhere evil appeared to triumph, even in the hearts of the so-called great Christian nations.

In spite of this disillusionment, the promise of the kingdom of God remains a biblical truth. Though the expectation that we ourselves will bring in the kingdom may be heresy, the promise of the kingdom is still one of the most powerful themes in the gospels.

As a key expression of this motif, Luke 7:18-23 can help us to recapture an appropriate theological understanding of the kingdom of God for Christian life, particularly in an urban setting.

> The disciples of John told him of all these things. And John, calling to him two of his disciples, sent them to the Lord, saying, "Are you he who is to come, or shall we look for another?" And when the men had come to him, they said, "John the Baptist has sent us to you, saying, 'Are you he who is to come or shall we look for another?' " In that hour he cured many of diseases and plagues and evil spirits, and on many that were blind

19

he bestowed sight. And he answered them, "Go and tell John what you have seen and heard: the blind receive their sight, the lame walk, lepers are cleansed, and the deaf hear, the dead are raised up, the poor have good news preached to them. And blessed is he who takes no offense at me."

In many senses, John's life was a unique human experience. Even before his birth John the Baptist had been chosen to proclaim the coming Messiah, and he had poured his whole life into this calling. When Jesus presented himself at the River Jordan, John the Baptist knew beyond doubt that this was the one for whom his entire life had prepared the way—the Messiah, indeed. Then, as John completed the baptism of Jesus, the heavens opened and God spoke the great confirmation, "This is my beloved Son, in whom I am well pleased." Probably few of us will ever experience a comparable sense of authentic vocation.

But several years later, in Luke, chapter 7, John is in prison under sentence of death at the whim of a jealous woman. Deeply troubled because Jesus is not behaving according to expectations, he sends his disciples to Jesus with a very simple question: "Our master John wants to know, are you the Messiah or shall we look for another?" Jesus responds gently, "Look around you. See the signs of *Shalom*. These are signs of the way God intends his kingdom to be." These same signs of *shalom* are found in the midst of daily life when men and women live in a relationship of love, obedience, and servanthood to God; when their relationships with each other express the reality of *agape*, that is, mutual love and self-giving; and when they relate to the earth as faithful stewards and not as exploiters. It was to signs such as these that Jesus pointed when John's disciples asked for reassurance. Wherever God's presence was manifest in Jesus, there the first fruits of the kingdom appeared, bringing new possibilities for all men and women. This is the ministry that Jesus gave to the church, his body. Where the church is, there by the grace of God we find signs of the kingdom. In these places shalom is made visible, experienced and proclaimed as urgently as if Jesus himself were present.

MISUNDERSTANDINGS OF THE KINGDOM

The importance and urgency of the kingdom of God have been interpreted differently by the various traditions of the church. One scheme of course, is the social gospel of Rauschenbush, distorted into an expectation that human efforts might ultimately bring in the kingdom. This illusion continues to be a key motif in far too much of Christian social concern. During the first part of the twentieth century a whole generation of clergy crusaded against the major social evils—racism, inadequate housing, abuse of civil liberties, and war—only to find themselves bitter and disillusioned at the end of their lives because they seemed to have made so little difference in the dimensions of these problems. This kind of disillusionment will continue to haunt our efforts to bring in the kingdom. The New Testament clearly teaches that Jesus defeated the principalities and powers of evil, and it is equally plain that our first duty is to integrate that victory in our lives. However, while we are to resist the evil which persists so strongly in the world, it is not within our power to totally eradicate it.

A second historical alternative is the Anabaptist pattern. Convinced that Luther was far too modest in his reforms, the left wing of the Reformation set out to recapture the essence of Christian community and witness. Their readings of the Scripture led them to conclude that they were called to live now a community of believers in order to be a concrete expression of the kingdom of God in the midst of an evil world. But the price of this commitment was to isolate themselves from the larger society as the Amish and other sectarian groups have done. These sect patterns appear to offer little help in relating the kingdom to an urban setting. But just as the social gospel was a powerful reminder of the importance of the kingdom to the church in previous days, so the Anabaptists make a powerful witness by their insistence upon commitment, accountability, and community.

A third option in the history of the church has been what Ernst Troeltsch called the "church type" relationship between communities of faith and the larger culture. This is classically reflected by the Protestant state churches of England and Scandinavia and by the Catholic tradition in France, Italy, and Spain. By its acceptance as the religious arm of the state, the European church has sought to create a genuine Christian culture and to maintain its role as the partner of secular authority. In this sense the church at its best can be a national conscience assuming responsibility for the moral attitudes and the Christian nurture of the society as a whole.

Troeltsch in his classic study, and H. Richard Niebuhr in *Christ and Culture,* have both defended the legitimacy of the various ways by which European churches relate to their own cultures, whether as sectarian groups or as national churches (or in other variations which Niebuhr addresses in his book). It might be said, however, that when European churches, either the sectarian or the state-church type were transposed to the United States, North American Christians created a new phenomenon, namely, denominations that combine the worst of both. That is, they retain the weaknesses of both the state church and the sect types, while offering the values and unique contributions of neither. On the one hand, North American denominations, by their insistence on the separation of church and state, have largely wasted their potential role as conscience of the state and nurturer of its common life. On the other hand, they have also failed to incorporate the crucial emphases of commitment, discipline, and accountability which made the sects such powerful witnesses to the renewing power of the kingdom.

A more balanced understanding of the kingdom of God might allow us to recapture the strength of both traditions. The practical outgrowth of this new interpretation would be a community of men and women deeply committed to Jesus Christ as Lord, who are prepared to let that commitment direct their lives, and are willing to be accountable to one another. In contrast to earlier sectarian models, however, the purpose of the new community will be to care for God's world and to be signs of the kingdom in the midst of human history rather than separated from it.

Nevertheless, at least for the present, the prospects for this type of community are most discouraging. In white middle-class suburban congregations the church seems to be only one interest in a life with many others, as though religion were simply one of the twenty-two departments in *Time* magazine. It seems that many people are prepared to attend church regularly only as long as it demands minimal time and energy. Most suburban pastors try to limit their sermons to twenty minutes so that church services will be out in an hour. What a contrast to the inner city where many black and Hispanic churches experience corporate worship as occasions for celebration and rejoicing in services that are both exciting and personally engrossing. At New York City's Canaan Baptist Church the Sunday service starts promptly at 10:45 and ends somewhere between 1:15 and 1:30. One senses not frustration at the length of the service, but rather a sense of genuine participation, new insights, and the presence and power of the Holy Spirit. In light of this enthusiasm, it would seem that the mainline church holds relatively little significance for great sectors of the white Protestant community. Nevertheless, we do not suggest that the inner-city church is without shortcomings. Churches that exhibit one sign of the kingdom are often weak in others, so we need to be clear about just what signs of the kingdom are actually the most urgent for today.

One of the most important of these signs appears to be evidence of personal and spiritual growth. As members of the church, Christians are all part of a community designed to nurture growth toward maturity in Christ. But most join the church and participate in its life for many years without necessarily experiencing significant change. Ephesians states that Christians are to grow to the measure of the stature and fullness of Christ; this is the maturity to which God calls us all. The context for this kind of growth is a Christian community that both sustains believers and challenges them. For Christians this is a lifelong process since no one ever attains the complete fullness of Christ. It is in this most personal sense that growth is urgently needed in churches today. If one were to ask most church members how their lives had progressed toward maturity in Christ during the last twelve months, it is probably safe to assume that few would have anything of significance to share.

It is thus quite appalling that so many denominations these days define church growth primarily in terms of either gaining new church members or developing new congregations. This misuse of the term would strip the local congregation of its potential to be a sign of the kingdom by dismissing a crucial work of the Holy Spirit. It is our contention that church growth, quite simply and unambiguously, is the task of nurturing each community of faith.

Another distressing outcome of this misuse of church growth is that it makes something of a travesty of evangelism. This is so, not as much because evangelism is sometimes used to bolster falling church membership in mainline denominations, but more because evangelism is presented in terms of a need for positive results, a teaching inconsistent with the spirit of the New Testament. Throughout the biblical record the church is directed to witness to the Lordship of Christ and to the presence of the kingdom. But there is a big difference between the word "witness" and the word "win." When one tells typical middle-class North Americans to "witness" for Christ, such persons will almost invariably hear "win" instead. The task as they understand it is to compel men and women into the kingdom. If they succeed, increases reflect mere numerical gain since there is little follow-up in qualitative Christian growth. At best these practices tend to short-circuit the godly pattern by which the Holy Spirit calls men and women to faith as they encounter the body of Christ. In a theological lecture on the meaning of evangelism, Paul Tillich said that the job of the evangelist was so to make visible Christ's body that men and women would make an honest decision for or against him. The evangelist, then, was not judged by his or her ability to win others, but by the faithfulness of the witness that led to the decision. Tillich also observed that many people who attend church have never authentically encountered Christ and accepted him as Lord, while many others who reject the church think they have said no to Jesus. The real issue for both is an honest exposure to the kingdom that would lead either to a real yes or a real no.

But our point here is the importance of the local church community to challenge and empower its members to maturity in Christ. The problems are all too obvious. One serious drawback is that Christians are far more inclined to view the church as a hospital rather than as a schoolhouse. Just as chaplains are usually the first resort when personal problems arise in the military, so in the minds of many people the church is primarily a source of consolation and help during life's crises. According to the New Testament, one key function of counseling is to equip men and women for their work as Christ's servants. Nevertheless, most clergy tend to spend most of their time counseling people with personal problems. As Bonhoeffer pointed out, pastors need to see themselves in a new role, not simply as ministers to people in their weakness, but more as agents of change to empower men and women in their Christian vocation.

Another problem associated with the concept of the church as a source of spiritual growth is the assumption that Christian education is primarily for children. Joining the church seems to be tantamount to graduation day and most new church members assume the status of Sunday school alumni. For many the idea that education continues throughout life comes as something of a shock. While many churchgoers will attend five weeks of Lenten school or a Bible study class on Sunday morning, the idea of a serious educational commitment is not exactly normative. The price of growth, new learning, and insight is pain, hard work, discipline, and struggle, yet few are prepared to see their local church as a setting for that kind of effort.

A further difficulty is that most people do not continue to learn or grow apart from a community that demands accountability and that helps to formalize commitments to spiritual discipline. No one has made the point more clearly than John Wesley. He insisted that new believers immediately become part of a class meeting where they would be nurtured in their new life in Christ, disciplined in those habits which would confirm their new commitment, and held accountable for their servanthood. Experience shows that the integrity of the Christian community is seriously jeopardized without this communal nurture, discipline, and accountability.

A final obstacle to realizing this potential for growth in the local church is that there is no common definition of Christian maturity. The long-standing debates between those who are once born and those who are twice born, between those who experience a dramatic conversion and those who apparently grow in Christ in a natural, progressive way, are expressions of this confusion. In recent years there has been a good deal of research on individual faith pilgrimages and the processes of spiritual growth. Some of the most helpful work has been done by John Westerhoff, a professor at Duke University, who studied the lives of several hundred Christian saints. Westerhoff suggests that faith maturity goes through four separate stages, without assurance that any one person will necessarily reach the fourth stage which is itself always open to continuing growth. He uses the images of rings on a tree. The first stage of faith is authentic and appropriate like the innermost ring on a tree which then may expand to a second or third or fourth ring. Thus he does not speak of authentic faith and inauthentic faith, but rather in terms of mature or partial faith growth.

The first stage, normative for small children, is what he refers to as "experienced" faith. This stage is typified by the small child who finds his or her place in the Christian community, who rejoices in the crèche at Christmas and in the other celebrations of the Christian year, who loves to hear the stories of faith, and who responds to the warmth and nurture of the church community.

The second ring encompasses the period of perhaps eight years through adolescence, when the important matters of faith concern participation in the Christian community. Westerhoff describes this stage as "the affiliate of faith" and it is illustrated by the young persons who genuinely enjoy the camaraderie and life of the Christian community, and who participate enthusiastically in junior-high youth groups and summer youth camps. This is an authentic level of faith, but it consists primarily of activity within the Christian community. It is at this point, according to Westerhoff, that young people are normally encouraged to join the church through confirmation or baptism. This process might better be described as church affiliation rather than as integration into the true body of Christ. He suspects that the overwhelming number of church members end faith pilgrimage here. Having joined the church they have nothing better to do than to criticize the younger generation and to accept passively the responsibilities and ministries of the church without moving on to any genuine sense of vocation in Christ.

The third stage occurs most appropriately in adolescence, but it must take place somewhere along the path if one is to go beyond the third ring. This he refers to as "questioning faith." It is the period when young people need to stand back from the values and beliefs inherited from parents, schools, and churches in order to establish their own adulthood and faith commitments. Erik Erikson refers to this step as the psycho-sexual moratorium; that is, the necessary springboard from adolescence to maturity. Young people in this stage ask the hard questions about faith. They need freedom to question and challenge established dogmas in order to discover what they themselves believe and what values they will adopt to define their own personhood. Westerhoff is quite convinced that without genuine questioning of faith, without honest effort to look at the important values of life and to establish a sense of individual identity, it is impossible for religious people to attain the maturity that leads to the fourth stage. This he calls "owned faith," a determination that Christ will indeed be Lord, and a commitment to allow that belief to shape the whole of life. In other words, identity in Christ now comes to mean sharing God's concern for the world and being signs of the kingdom in the church and in the world. It seems likely that part of the reason for the great departure of Roman Catholic and Protestant clergy from the church during the 1960s relates to this understanding of the faith pilgrimage. Many of these clergy decided on their vocation as early as fourteen or fifteen years of age, and then continued on through high school, denominational college, and seminary without ever having experienced the questioning which leads to owned faith.

Thus we stress our first point. The church is a powerful sign of the kingdom, authentically the body of Christ, when the world encounters it as a community of believers whose lives are continually growing toward maturity, who are living examples of men and women on the way to the stature of Christ, willing to undergo the pain, discipline, and hard work which that requires. Clearly this will only happen if Christians stop insisting that the church exists to meet their personal needs and begin seeing it as a schoolhouse of faith which challenges and empowers them to exercise their creative potential in God's service even in the midst of their frailty. It is time to stop recruiting members by telling them what great things the church will do for them without ever implying that the church will above all assist them in living obedient and faithful lives. A congregation whose members are on fire with faith, whose lives are exciting and growing, who have the courage to face whatever challenge comes in the confidence that Christ is Lord is a powerful sign of the kingdom to a jaded, bored, anxious, and frustrated world. This is the kind of sign that virtually forces nonbelievers to find out what is going on. It gives the church today the chance to demonstrate the kingdom as Jesus once did.

SIGNS OF THE KINGDOM: THE UNITY OF THE BODY OF CHRIST

The second sign of the kingdom is more poignant and troubling. A sign that is urgently needed in our day is a community of faith that reflects unity in Christ, a gathering that cuts across the terrible divisions not only between denominations but more especially between ethnic and class groups in North American society. Early in its life the East Harlem Protestant Parish faced this problem. The denomination originally refused funding for the parish because officials did not see East Harlem as a mission community. Those in power made it quite clear that from their perspective all Puerto Ricans were Roman Catholics, and that all blacks in the community went uptown to Harlem churches. According to them, there was no urgency about any religious ministry in that neighborhood. When they were informed that most people in East Harlem didn't go to church at all, the denominations responded by saying "they're not our kind of people." This was not meant in a derogatory sense but merely reaffirmed the tendency of denominations in this country to look for people who logically belong in their nets. There was no one in East Harlem from Scotland for the Presbyterians. There were no Scandinavians who would logically be Lutheran and no New Englanders who belonged in a Congregational church. In other words, none of the major denominations felt much responsibility because of a basic North American assumption that most people belong in a particular church. What we call evangelism almost invariably turns out to be either church extension, that is, providing new churches for members who move out of the city, or some form of revivalism that brings people back to their former faith or to a community of faith to which they once belonged. Neither is evangelism in the biblical sense.

The East Harlem Parish began to consider whether to cater to the black community and start black churches, or whether to concentrate on the Hispanic community and minister to them in Spanish churches. But having never heard of the homogeneous unit principle, in the end they set out to prove that in the little storefront churches of the parish, blacks and Hispanics and whites, people with college degrees and those who had not finished grade school, people of all sorts and all conditions could find a new community. This approach is not likely to produce large congregations, but it is nonetheless a crucial witness to the kingdom. When these parish Christians gather around the communion table with a loaf of Italian bread that somebody has bought on the way to church, and then break the bread together with the words "because there is one loaf, we who are many are one body, for we all partake of the same loaf," one sometimes actually senses that by the grace of God these people are more truly brothers and sisters and aunts and uncles than any flesh and blood. What an incredible sign of the kingdom, experiencing firsthand the biblical reality that in Christ there is neither Jew nor Gentile, male nor female, ethnic minority nor white, rich nor poor, but all are made one in him.

When the outside community looks through the windows of those congregations they are troubled in heart. They may be baffled or upset or angry or curious, but they definitely want to find out what is going on, for they know only too well that Puerto Ricans don't belong with blacks or whites, and that blacks prefer their own churches. Genuine signs of the kingdom today are likely to be every bit as unnerving as Pentecost. The struggle for unity is always hard. One of the most serious difficulties is creating meaningful styles of worship for culturally diverse congregations. But in Christ the new church family can develop appropriate new traditions. When a city like New York, rife with social dissension, sees formerly hostile constituents living together in harmony, the political implications are staggering. Jesus prayed that "they may be one even as we are one, I in them and thou in me, that they may become perfectly one, so that the world may know that thou hast sent me and hast loved them even as thou hast loved me" (John 17:22,23). The church's claim to represent the kingdom will not be taken seriously until it models the unity of Christ in a broken world.

For this reason it is most disheartening that many mainline white denominations now appear to have given up the struggle against racism and sexism. White congregations seem to be convinced that such great progress was made during the 1960s and 1970s that the problem of racism no longer exists. One possible explanation for this gross misunderstanding is that the civil rights movement and civil rights legislation did open new doors to a significant percentage of the black community. One now expects to find black lawyers in white firms, black doctors in white hospitals, and black families in white suburban neighborhoods. In other words, perhaps 25 percent of the black community now enjoys access to the world of the white middle class. In this relatively specialized sector are the people our white brothers and sisters have come to know and recognize. From the perspective of this black minority, there have been tremendous changes in business and social communities in the last ten or fifteen years. What is hidden from the eyes of white North America is that for an even larger percentage of black men and women in this country, the gap between black and white has steadily increased in the last twenty years. In a brilliant lecture at the 1979 annual meeting of the Urban League, civil rights leader Vernon Jordan presented dramatic evidence that most blacks in urban centers have actually lost ground in terms of education, jobs, housing, health, and other key indicators of status in North America. This is the tragic reality that we have so carelessly overlooked.

It is now almost painfully clear that the evil of racism is not exclusive to the South. Before 1965 or so, one did not refer to Harlem as a ghetto because by definition the North didn't have a race problem. Still, when Martin Luther King came to Chicago he noted that people like Bull Connor ought to come to Chicago because up there they really knew how to hate. What greater violation of the kingdom can there be than for a society to deny men and women the opportunity to fulfill their potential as children of God simply on the basis of color?

In the same way, sexism also disrupts the unity that Christ offers his church. In recent years, the United Church of Christ ordained nearly 500 women, more even than the United Methodist Church. Nevertheless, of those 500 only 32 became congregational pastors in their own right, and as one might expect, their parishes lay in the far reaches of North Dakota, Vermont, and Idaho where male candidates were unwilling to serve. In effect, the church ordains women only to refuse their qualifications. This practice continues even though women are now recognized as some of the ablest students at many first-rate seminaries. It is no easy thing for a liberated woman to become a Christian. It takes a while to discover that Jesus was a feminist and that St. Paul, in his own cultural context, upheld the worth of women. But once that decision is made it is even harder for a woman to adopt a responsible vocation within the life of the church.

As the church works to extinguish both racism and sexism, white North American Christians must also guard against what might be called the white liberal syndrome. According to a black colleague, "White liberals are white men and women deeply committed to help their black brothers and sisters, willing to go to Selma, get busted, and go to jail. They are prepared to deal with the problem of racism and stand loud and clear against injustice, but they are still benefitting from the privileges which come through the system of racism. A white liberal is one who helps his less fortunate black brother but doesn't face his implications as part of the problem."

27

A congregation struggling to overturn principalities and powers in the form of racism and sexism is a powerful sign of the kingdom. In the other direction, the homogeneous unit principle that suggests that the most effective model of evangelism is the appeal to homogeneous racial classes and social groups seems to come dangerously close to endorsing these two evils.

On such grounds the homogeneity principle and the idea of church expansion as a definition of evangelism appear to border on heresy. Yet one still finds among advocates of both of these practices men and women whose lives genuinely reflect the spirit of Christ. Under these conditions, one is not entirely comfortable with the finding of heresy. It may be that both the church growth movement and its corollary, the homogeneous unit principle, first developed in response to the particular needs of foreign missions in countries where these patterns do not violate the integrity of the church. Perhaps these are indeed legitimate patterns for work in other lands. Nevertheless, these same concepts applied to a secularized church in a pseudo-Christian culture can only be disastrous both for the church and for North American society as a whole.

SIGNS OF THE KINGDOM: SERVANTHOOD

The third convincing sign of the kingdom is servanthood. When the world looks at congregations it needs to see people whose caring extends beyond the local church body. The Gospel assumes that congregations are families and that families watch out for each other. But the Gospel also frees us to take care of God's world. Hoekendijk put it neatly: "The church unlike any other human community, is ex-centric."

According to Genesis, God made the most beautiful world possible, and then he created human beings to enjoy it and have charge over it. The thing that truly makes life worthwhile (or abundant as Jesus put it) is having nothing better to do than to take care of God's world. In this vocation we may employ all of our energy, our gifts, and our dreams. The church is the strategic base that helps equip us and deploy us, revive us and renew us, to hold that vision before us and to expound that joy for our understanding. Martin Luther once said that until Christ is truly Lord, we will worry about ourselves, and that even our participation in the church is geared towards meeting our personal needs. But when Christ is Lord, we are turned inside out so that our first concern is to be Christ to our neighbors. Most Christians today have a long way to go to demonstrate this kind of extended concern. The church that stops worrying about interior maintenance because it is so busy taking care of God's world is a welcome sign of the kingdom.

Still, even when churches are willing to exercise servanthood, they often overlook the pitfall of the Good Samaritan story. Like most parables it makes a very useful point. If we apply it to our own day, however, the story suggests some wider implications for the modern good neighbor. For example, suppose that on his way to work on Monday our contemporary Samaritan stops to assist a robbery victim and doesn't get to work until three o'clock in the afternoon. After hearing his story, the boss responds, "That's a very moving thing you did," and doesn't even charge him with a sick day. When the story is repeated on Tuesday, however, he gets docked a day's pay, and by Thursday when the same thing has happened four days in a row, he is out of a job. At some point it might occur to this well-intentioned soul that the real problem was police protection on the Jericho Road.

The church will have to be content with rescuing the same victims day after day unless it begins to confront what the New Testament so aptly calls the "principalities and powers which do beset us so heavily." Many evangelical conservatives tend to assume that social action is wrong and political involvement is evil. But when one begins to wrestle with the passages in Colossians and Ephesians about principalities and powers, one begins to understand that the evils Paul is talking about are embodied in the Board of Education, the United Federation of Teachers, the Democratic Party, the United Methodist Church, the United Church of Christ, and the AMA.

The key prophetic task of the clergy today is neither to foretell the future nor to initiate social action, but rather to sound the indictment of Isaiah 58:1-9a. "Cry aloud, spare not . . . declare to my people their transgression, to the house of Jacob their sins. Yet they . . . delight to know my ways, as if they were a nation that did righteousness" (vv.1,2a). If the religious community can come to appreciate the enormous gap between profession and reality, between faith and practice, the Holy Spirit may begin to work and God's people may yet become powerful signs of the kingdom.

CONCLUSION

As Christians, we are called to be signs of the kingdom through communities that model unity, nurture growth, and promote servanthood. We do not strive to bring in the kingdom of God, but rather to be signs of the kingdom in a world under the power of evil. Thus we are prepared for conflict and struggle. At this moment in North American history, it is important that the church adopt what Niebuhr has called a Christ against culture perspective. Certainly many of the values of contemporary North American society—the race to stockpile the world's largest arsenal, the good life defined in terms of TV commercials, and the large-scale institutionalization of racism and sexism—are far from the New Testament ideal. But when we urge a Christ against culture perspective, we do so in the sense of that remarkable text in Jeremiah 29, where the prophet reminds the exiles in Babylon to "Seek the *shalom* of the city where I have sent you into exile" (v.7). Here, then, is the point of opposition, the recognition that as Christians we are in a significant sense exiles in our own land. But Jeremiah goes on: "And pray to the Lord on its behalf. For in seeking its shalom you will find your shalom." Thus the church stands apart from and against society neither to preserve its own purity nor to provide an escape from the tensions of exile, but rather so that we may find the very purpose of our lives as we seek the *shalom* of the cities where God has placed us as servants. God desperately needs those in the midst of our cities who are both prophets to expose the injustice of North American society and ministers to care for its victims.

There is a parting footnote here for my colleagues in the professional ministry. Most pastors are evaluated (and indeed, evaluate themselves) in terms of their role as a skilled preacher. But what if our first calling were to be a rabbi? Jesus, you will remember, was called rabbi more than anything else. To be a rabbi in this sense would mean helping those who come to hear us preach on Sunday to begin to grow toward maturity in Christ and to empower them to be willing to undergo the pain and hard work of discipleship. Perhaps a truer measure of ministry than the power of our sermons might be the growth in faith of our congregations.

It may also be time to redefine ministry in terms of another key pastoral role, that of social action leader. In the past we clergy found ourselves at the head of the troops, leading the fight against racial oppression and the war in Vietnam. Suppose instead that we were called to be *community organizers* and that our skills were to be those of an Alinsky-type leader: mobilizing church resources, developing leadership potential in the congregation, and dispersing men and women into the city both to challenge the principalities and powers of society and to help heal the casualties of modern urban life. What if the test of our ministry were not the quality of our own social action but the level of community involvement among our local members?

THE FUTURE—ON EARTH AS IT IS IN HEAVEN

Thomas W. Sine, Jr., researcher and planner, World Concern

The decade of the 1980s is being recognized as the decade of the poor, particularly the urban poor. The urban explosion now underway in the Third World will peak with Mexico City as the world's largest city with 32 million people, and Sao Paulo, Brazil, as second with 25 million. Most of this growth will accrue from urban immigration. Newcomers to the city will settle into squatter communities that offer no life-support systems in terms of sanitation, health services, and food distribution. The potential for disaster in Third World cities is building day by day.

The North American city is not without its own problems. One increasingly critical area is that of housing. Jim Wallis of *Sojourners* predicts that by 1984, there will be 100,000 displaced people in Washington, D.C.

This grim forecast is compounded by the virtual certainty of rising food and energy costs. Many city dwellers already have to choose between food and heating. Those on fixed incomes are especially vulnerable, but the younger middle class may be equally hard hit. Most urban planners see increasing shortages of jobs, food, housing, and energy as realities of the future. Still, by creative thinking and inventive planning, the church might revise or at least forestall some of these projections.

What we want to focus on here is how we might use the future as a context for building a theology that can guide our thinking about urban ministry.

To begin, let us consider two interrelated questions: What is your image of the ideal future and where does that image come from? There is actually quite a rich heritage of images in North American culture, but most people would not be able to pinpoint a particular image as the basis for their own personal vision. Thus some historical background will be helpful before we move into a discussion of a biblical perspective. Some of these images of the ideal future concern the United States as a whole; others relate more directly to the city per se.

One of the earliest visions of the New World's potential appeared in 1630. John Winthrop stood on the foredeck of the *Arabella* and proclaimed, "People, we are on a mission of unqualified importance. God has called us to build a 'city on a hill.' Nothing less. The eyes of all the world are upon

31

us." These people saw themselves neither as colonists nor as religious refugees, but as builders of the millennial kingdom of Christ. They believed that Christ would return only when the church was purified, and saw their chance to build a righteous society in an unspoiled environment that would challenge the church in Europe to follow suit. This vision of North America as the "city on a hill" is our first image.

Tied closely into the preceding image was the vision of North America as a new Eden. For centuries Europe had been overrun with wars, feudalism, and urban decay. Barring some difficulties with the indigenous population, this new continent appeared to offer a second chance to return to the innocence of Eden. Such romantic visions were replete throughout early North American literature.

Another important early image was the notion of North Americans as a people empowered by their connection to the land. Thomas Jefferson believed that landed farmers were the strength of the nation. His hopes for the United States were inseparably joined to a pastoral vision of the future. Throughout most of our early history, many American thinkers, including Poe, Thoreau, and Emerson, saw the city as anything but positive. If North America were the millennial kingdom, the landed gentry were the children of God.

Benjamin Franklin rejected this static vision. He saw the United States as a nation of people on the move and lobbied vigorously for progress and urban development. To him the open frontier was an invitation to national expansion, and his first choice to develop this new territory was the rising middle class. As our first urbanologist, Franklin encouraged population growth, and his population forecasts were accurate through about 1850. He was unquestionably the most aggressive and creative urban planner in early North America.

Edward Bellamy carried Franklin's bias one step further. In his 1877 novel, *Looking Backwards,* he depicted the city as utopia. Bellamy was disturbed by the frequent riots, oppression, and human suffering of nineteenth-century Boston. In his book, Jeremy West goes to sleep in A.D. 1877 and wakes up in the ideal Boston of A.D. 2000. Since Bellamy was a professing Christian, it is not surprising that the foundations of his ideal city are equal opportunity and meaningful work. What is somewhat unexpected is that these utopian objectives are achieved solely through government intervention and bureaucratic planning. Interestingly enough, at least part of his vision has been fulfilled by the passage of federal equal opportunity legislation.

A more recent image, pursued by futurist Herman Kahn and other contemporary thinkers, is that of the city as a generator of progress, a technological dynamo. They see the North American city as it appears in Sandburg's "Chicago"—a powerful giant whose vigor and industry are boundless. In their scheme, science and technology under urban leadership will initiate a new egalitarian North American society.

This vision serves as the foundation for our final image, that of the North American city as "last chance." Unlike the others, this is not an indigenous image; it belongs to the Third World poor. Life in our cities is recognized worldwide as the highest expression of consumerism, affluence, and technological progress. Individuals and families swarm into these depots believing that if they can just get close enough to it, the American dream will be theirs. What even many Americans refuse to acknowledge is that current resources cannot indefinitely support U.S. affluence. Of all the images considered so far, this is potentially the most bankrupt.

For most Americans, Thomas Jefferson's ideal of the United States as a pastoral paradise has all but eclipsed other historical images. On the whole, the church tends to share the prejudice that cities are unnatural and unwholesome. Those Christians who identify a better future with country living have serious problems with a hopeful view of the city. One exercise that is often used in future workshops is to have participants design an ideal habitat ten years in the future. For Christians, this setting is almost invariably rural.

One eschatological perspective not uncommon among theological conservatives can be summarized somewhat crudely as, "If things don't get worse, Jesus won't come." The logical implication of this line of thinking is that Christians could hasten Christ's return by cancelling relief programs and actively promoting social unrest. Let us be clear: this is not acceptable theology, this is escapism. This eschatological perversion immobilizes us and compromises our response to the genuine biblical mission.

As an alternative to this escapism, many other Christians carelessly align themselves with any organization that seems to promote social change. In their concern for the city and for more appropriate and adequate delivery systems of human services, they fail to question the value systems behind these programs. These unexamined agendas may be controlled by images of growth, utopianism, and social progress rather than by concerns for human dignity and well-being.

Both those who are waiting for their own escape and those who work, albeit thoughtlessly, for social change, may also operate under another set of values that tends to constrict their ability to discern and respond to theological issues. The narcissistic preoccupation of North American culture has penetrated the church fully as much as any other organization, to the extent that some Christians spend more time praying for parking spaces than for children starving in Cambodia.

The conservative religious community seems to be constantly on guard against the evils of secular humanism. A far greater danger, however, lies in the fact that our faith has already been compromised by the individualistic materialism of North American culture. Such attitudes lead U.S. Christians to hoard resources that could be shared with the world's hungry, dispossessed, and helpless. If it were possible to inventory the total collective wealth of North American Christians including property, time, talents, and finances and then compare this gross figure to the amount actually channeled to relief efforts of any kind, we might well be appalled.

The Bible is quite clear about God's vision of the future. This powerful image first comes to light in his promise to Abraham: "In you all the nations of the world are going to be blessed." It broadens in the promise of the rainbow, and in the hope of the promised land. The promised land is meant to symbolize God's intention to one day bring his people into a new place, a new future. The image is further developed in the jubilee Scripture which establishes the groundwork for a society based on justice, redistribution of wealth and property, and remembrance of the poor. Isaiah 9 completes the picture. Oppression is gone forever. The new society is one of peace where the garments rolled in blood from warfare are thrown in the fire for burning. Best of all a child is born to be our king and of the increase and peace of his government there shall be no end. A kingdom of peace, justice, and hope—this is God's design for our future.

Another exciting Old Testament image of the future appears in Isaiah 60. It tells of a towering mountain in a vast desert. On top of this mountain in the city of New Jerusalem a glorious party is in progress. At this feast are people from every tongue and tribe and nation, with more streaming in all the time. This celebration marks the beginning of a new age in which God wipes away all tears and puts an end to all human suffering. Now that God reigns with his people, New Jerusalem is all justice, hope, peace, and righteousness. The city itself has been redeemed.

We might think of the New Testament as God's overture of the world to come and the life, ministry, and servanthood of Jesus as the dominant strains of the future. Every time Jesus heals the sick, feeds the hungry, and liberates the oppressed, we experience what life will be like in the promised kingdom of righteousness, peace, and justice. But Jesus taught us to pray, "Thy kingdom come, thy will be done on earth as it is in heaven . . . ."

It seems a tragic mistake to assign the kingdom to the other side of the apocalypse, when the church has all the information it needs to start building that kingdom right now. As Christians we can choose to work with God to transform the cities of the world.

One way to begin would be to seek God's vision for our particular community. Once we share this vision, we can ask the Holy Spirit to help us innovate urban ministries to meet human needs more effectively. At the same time we can probably expect less support than before from federal, state, and even church resources. Instead of centralized ministry programs, we may have to consider more individualized responses—moving back into city neighborhoods, looking for jobs in the city, and developing more specialized ministries keyed to local needs. It will almost certainly mean reevaluating our use of materials and buildings.

Every time we work for righteousness, peace, and justice, we affirm that kingdom which is both here now and is to come. However it is present now, in small signs or great, we need to rejoice. One day we will be with God in a new city where there is only cause for celebration. "Our Father, who art in heaven, hallowed be thy name, thy kingdom come . . . ."

THEOLOGICAL
PERSPECTIVES

A REFORMED THEOLOGICAL PERSPECTIVE ON POLITICS

Richard W. Mouw, professor, Calvin College

There was a time, not too long ago, when it was possible to develop a Reformed theological perspective on this subject or that as if the endeavor needed no further justification. Labels such as Reformed, Catholic, Lutheran, Mennonite, and Wesleyan, along with liberal, conservative, and neo-orthodox, were taken as the most appropriate way of dividing up the confessional-theological terrain.

But these tags are no longer the most common theological currency. Today it is much more likely that people will describe their theologies as feminist or black or Hispanic or Asian or liberation. The use of these kinds of modifiers is meant to criticize the older way of choosing up sides. Some contemporary thinkers now dismiss traditional theologies as seriously, perhaps hopelessly, compromised by white, Western, even North Atlantic interests and concerns.

This is an important and to a large degree legitimate criticism. Theologizing does not occur in a racial, sexual, political, or economic vacuum, but is greatly influenced by the social context from which it emerges. And it is simply a fact that theologizing has been controlled by the white-male dominated North Atlantic community.

But traditional positions are not so simply discounted. For one thing, many of the issues on which historical theologies are based just will not go away—at least they have not gone away yet. The world-wide Christian community is still divided in its thinking about sacraments, ecclesiastical authority, the Scriptures, faith and reason, and the relationship between the church and the world.

Indeed, in reading the work of contextualized theologians one has the distinct impression that the older traditions and categories are still matters of importance. Gustavo Gutierrez strikes me as a distinctively Catholic theologian; Jose Miguez-Bonino appears more Protestant in his thinking. Some feminists seem to be very liberal theologically, while others are more conservative. And James Cone, even in the midst of his careful and loving examination of traditional black spirituality (best seen in *The Spirituals and the Blues*), appears at points to be a strongly Tillichian black theologian.

All this is not to suggest that the older labels retain their legitimacy at the

37

expense of newer ways of identifying theological positions. Both approaches have important things to say to the church.

In using the term Reformed this paper does mean to appeal to a distinctive core of Reformed emphases. But this should in no way imply a lack of appreciation for the significant advances made by recent contextualized theologies.

Theologians use the term Reformed in a narrower and a broader sense. The narrower sense has to do with Reformed emphases on soteriology or the doctrine of salvation. Here the focus is on the question of how an individual is saved.

Reformed, in the broader sense, has to do with a theology of culture. Here the label is closely aligned with the perspective on culture found in H. Richard Niebuhr's *Christ in Culture*. Reformed Christians have traditionally seen the divine command in Genesis 1, to fill the earth and have dominion over it, as a cultural mandate to develop social patterns and institutions in obedience to the will of God.

For Calvinists obedience to this cultural mandate is especially urgent under sinful conditions. They would argue, along with Abraham Kuyper that,"There is not an inch in the entire area of our human life of which Christ, who is sovereign of all, does not call 'Mine!' '' According to them it is the duty of the Christian community to work to transform all of human cultural activity.

We might call this broader Reformed perspective cultural Calvinism, as opposed to individual or soteriological Calvinism. In cultural Calvinism, as in all Reformed theology, the doctrine of God's sovereignty is central.

This teaching has long been key among Dutch and Scottish Calvinists, British and North American Puritans, and among the Afrikaners of South Africa. But it has often miscarried and, in the case of South Africa, now perversely reinforces overt injustice and oppression. At best it seems that cultural Calvinists have applied scriptural norms and mandates only selectively.

Politically, the Reformed community has rather consistently operated from a position of power. This is not to say that Calvinists have always enjoyed economic or political privilege, but they often have. Even as a relatively underprivileged minority their situation has seldom been as desperate as the truly powerless of history. The Puritans of England or the dissenting Calvinists in nineteenth-century Holland still had ways of being heard or putting pressure on a temporarily hostile system. They could legitimately plan for a better future.

One factor that contributes to Calvinism's failure to identify with the powerless is its discernible bias in favor of the political status quo. A favorite dogma of Reformed Christians is the need for order in human affairs. Since human beings are radically sinful, civil government serves in good part to combat the evil tendencies of human nature. Because Calvinism tends to expect practically the worst from individuals, little better is expected of governments. As a result, Reformed Christians have tolerated all kinds of unjust governments on the grounds that even bad governments promote a necessary order in the midst of human depravity.

38

This line of thinking has not gone unchallenged. Calvin himself contended that revolution on occasion, and under specified conditions, is legitimate. The Belgic Confession also stipulated that Christians are to obey civil magistrates "in all things which are not repugnant to the Word of God."

No Christian can offer unconditional obedience to a human government. That would be idolatry. The Reformed tradition acknowledges this in its official and quasi-official statements about the relationship between citizen and government. As a result, these statements consistently leave room for individuals to assess the legitimacy of governments and policies in light of Scripture.

At present, this potential for political critique remains undeveloped. It is at this point that the recent contextualized theologies mentioned earlier might enrich and renew Reformed thinking. This, in fact, is already happening in what is perhaps the world's largest community of politically oppressed Calvinists—the black Reformed church of South Africa. That community of approximately one and a half million believers shows signs of theological foment which could result in a genuinely Reformed theology of liberation. Allan Boesak, a black Reformed South African theologian, has produced a fascinating and brilliant statement of such a theological perspective in *Farewell to Innocence* (Orbis Books, 1976).

What do Calvinists mean when they speak of developing a theological perspective on politics? As commonly used the term has at least three senses. First, politics can be defined as the socially legitimized processes of decision-making and policy-setting in what we ordinarily think of as the civil arena. Here the stuff of politics includes the formal structures and activities of parliaments, congresses, presidential staffs, and city halls.

A second sense of politics relates to the broader public arena, in which groups, institutions, and individuals interact both with each other and with formal political structures. Ralph Nader, Jane Fonda, and Jesse Jackson have not gained their present positions by popular election. Still, in a larger sense, they are political figures representing political movements and causes.

A third sense of politics bears on decision-making processes and authority patterns in a wide variety of institutions. Thus we speak of church politics, university politics, and even family politics.

The Scriptures treat politics in all of these senses. Genesis describes the first human pair placed in Eden to have dominion together over the nonhuman creation. This shared dominion was quickly perverted by the willful attempt of Adam and Eve to "be like God, knowing good and evil." With their rebellion came competition, suspicion, and strife—the very seeds of political struggle.

Nevertheless, God was gracious. One of his first redemptive acts was to call together a nation through whom he might reintroduce himself to the world.

The corporate life of Old Testament Israel only foreshadowed a fuller redemption to come. Within this people arose a hope for one who would be the consolation of Israel, a hope that was expressed in many ways: a perfect sacrifice; a lamb without blemish and spot; a suffering servant; a son of man; and the ancient of days. But this hope also took a *political* form. In the midst of political disaster, Old Testament prophets proclaimed the coming of a righteous king whose reign would bring unceasing peace and prosperity; a liberator who would be a powerful ally of the widow, the sojourner, the prisoner, and the beggar.

The New Testament reveals that Israel's deepest yearnings were more than fulfilled in the ministry, death, and resurrection of Jesus.

The Reformed tradition, with its emphasis on covenant theology, has always insisted on the continuity of faith between Israel and the New Testament church. Reformed Christians have consistently argued against a dispensationalist hermeneutic, which assigns a physical, political destiny to Israel and a spiritual, other-worldly destiny to the church. At the heart of Calvinism has been the refusal of the thesis that in the Old Testament God dealt with a corporate entity, while in the New Testament he deals with individuals. Reformed Christianity, especially cultural Calvinism, contends that the Bible is one story, from beginning to end, so that believers of every age must give corporate expression to their faith.

One might spend a good deal of time exploring how these Reformed tenets inform our approach to current political concerns, or, more specifically, how they bear on *urban* political issues. Instead, we shall content ourselves with making the questions themselves more specific, in hopes that we will uncover some key issues along the way.

How do we relate theology to concrete political action? In asking this question we acknowledge that our course of action in developing an activist political theology is itself a problem for theological reflection. Plato once argued that philosopher-kings were the only appropriate rulers. When asked where he expected to find philosopher-kings, he replied that either philosophers were going to have to become kings, or kings were going to have to become philosophers. An analogous situation holds true here. Either those who are skilled in practical politics must become theologically minded, or theologians must become politically knowledgeable. At the very least, the concerned politicians and theologians will need to converse before the Word of God.

All this, of course, is only to describe how we might *begin* to formulate such a theological perspective, but such a beginning would be no small accomplishment. It would be somewhat like struggling with a new language until we could learn to speak in terms of urban political issues. What forces are at work in urban development and decay? What do actual urban budgets look like? Whose interests, either directly or indirectly, actually control the allocation of goods and funds in the city? Who profits from these allocations, and in what ways? Who suffers, and in what ways? Who are the urban planners? What does it feel like to live in an urban ghetto? What are the threats, frustrations, and perhaps rewards, of daily life for urban dwellers? What are the *actual*, as opposed to *official*, patterns of political power in the city?

With these and a host of other questions in mind we can search the Scriptures, theological studies, received traditions of the Christian community, and our own minds. If we can develop Christian sensitivities as we approach these questions, we might find unexpected ways for the Christian message to connect with issues of urban political life.

What is the destiny of the city, biblically understood? This question is fertile ground for urban-theological debate. Is there an eschatological perspective on the city? How does the city fit into the biblical vision of last things?

A full-scale investigation of this topic would reveal a number of conflicting opinions. In *The Secular City*, Harvey Cox is optimistic about the urbanization of modern life. He seems to affirm the basic forces at work in the city, even those forces that lead to increasing bureaucratization and anonymity. On the other hand, Jacques Ellul's *The Meaning of the City* is a lengthy jeremiad on the subject of urbanization. Ellul views the city in demonic terms: "the city breaks with the order of divine creation." For him, the city embodies human sinfulness and rebellion. The city stands under the divine curse.

In their strongest statements of their respective cases, Cox and Ellul stand at opposite ends of the spectrum; Cox optimistically embraces the modern city, Ellul rejects it. But each, in the course of the discussion, qualifies his case.

Interestingly enough, we find this same underlying ambivalence about the city in the Bible. In Revelation two cities, Babylon and Jerusalem, are prominent in the scenario of the final struggle between Christ and Antichrist. Babylon, with its corrupt merchants and politicians, and its oppression of the poor, is the urban embodiment of evil. It typifies all in urban life that stands under the divine curse. The very fact that such a portrayal exists in the Bible should be enough to deter Christians from a naïve optimism about the power of the city.

From a Reformed perspective this picture of Babylon is hardly surprising. Those who believe in personal total depravity have no difficulty with a city whose depravity is total. From the perspective of cultural Calvinism, it is to be expected that evil would be manifest in institutional, corporate life.

Nevertheless, those of us who espouse the transformational character of cultural Calvinism will insist that the potrayal of the New Jerusalem must also be reckoned with. As Ellul and others have pointed out, the story of the Bible begins in a garden and ends in a city. The final vision of the city is one of hope. The tree of life, first planted in Eden, now grows in the heart of the new Jerusalem. As an *urban* tree, it has sprouted leaves "for the healing of the nations."

The final course of history as seen in Revelation 21 and 22 is sweeping towards a city. It is fascinating to realize when John records this final vision he sees the need for a resolution of political struggle and abuse of power. Revelation 21:24, 26 states that, "the kings of the earth" will bring "the glory and the honor of the nations" into the new Jerusalem. This would seem to indicate that God will not destroy the products of human culture, "the glory and the honor of the nations," but will instead incorporate them into the city for his pleasure.

The kings referred to in these verses are not strictly political figures; they also represent the peoples of the earth in all their cultural diversity. But they are *at least* political, and their political power and authority will be gathered in at the last day. God's supreme authority will be formally acknowledged by all who have used and misused political power. There is a replay here of the theme of Philippians 2:10,11 "every knee should bow, in heaven and on earth and under the earth. . . to the glory of God the Father."

We find similar themes in the Old Testament, especially in Isaiah 60. Here too is a vision of a transfigured city that draws tokens of the cultural power from many nations: laden camels from Midian and Ephah and Sheba, cargo-heavy ships of Tarshish, and precious woods from Lebanon.

But here too are glimpses of political resolution. "Foreigners shall build up your walls, and their kings shall minister to you"; the city will receive the "wealth of the nations, with their kings led in procession"; "the sons of those who oppressed you shall come bending low to you"; "violence shall no more be heard in your land, devastation or destruction within your borders."

In short, the city is key to biblical visions of humanity's final destiny. Within the walls of the transformed city, political vindication is realized by those of many nations who are gathered into its shelter. Life here is justice and righteousness and peace. The biblical word about this kind of city is the ultimate word; all else that we read of corrupt cities in the grip of demonic powers is penultimate.

What is the relationship of the city, viewed eschatologically, to present urban realities? This is a crucial question. How should the biblical vision of the future shape our present attitudes and actions?

The relationship here is a complex one. Consider again the vision of Isaiah 60. We might think of this prophecy as being fulfilled in three different stages. The first stage has already occurred for Old Testament Israel. Yet it was for them only a partial and fragmentary realization. This Scripture promised the restoration of Jerusalem to Jews in exile or just returning from exile. They, or their children, were to rebuild Jerusalem as the home of God's chosen people and as a center of international commerce. Nevertheless this Jerusalem never really approached the grandeur of Isaiah's vision.

We might consider the New Testament church as the second stage of this fulfillment. Here the body of believers could be seen as a city drawing inhabitants from many nations. In this new city the gifts of many peoples are shared, power and authority are transformed, and oppression is lifted. This fulfills another part of Isaiah's promise: "You shall call your walls Salvation, and your gates Praise."

But the final denouement is yet to come. Until then the people of God await the city which shall embody the riches of their "Redeemer, the Mighty One of Jacob."

We, like Abraham, look "forward to a city which has foundations, whose builder and maker is God." Nevertheless, and this is key, we wait as those who are already delegates of that city. This is our time of exile, but even in exile we are still a holy nation and a royal priesthood under our King, Jesus Christ. Many of the blessings of the promised city are already ours, with more for the asking.

Now, what we hope for in the future city, and what we presently realize in the body of Christ, is also what God wants for all human beings. While we are called to witness to the coming of God's city, biblical visions of that city can also guide and inform our present efforts to establish urban justice and righteousness. We can legitimately work for the elimination of oppression and the transformation of culture as the first fruits of God's rule over the city.

What is the practical content of the phrase "urban justice"? Reformed thinkers have traditionally placed great emphasis on the legitimate exercise of civil authority. This emphasis is closely related to the concern, mentioned earlier, for the ordering of sinful human affairs, but it is certainly not unrelated to the traditional identification of the Reformed community with the political and economic status quo.

Nevertheless this emphasis, whether properly or improperly developed in the Reformed (or any other) tradition, is biblical. In Romans 13, Paul directs us to submit to political authority and Peter speaks of honoring the emperor in 1 Peter 2. These and other New Testament passages have a conservative bent which we cannot completely ignore.

On the other hand, subjection and honor are not to be confused with uncritical obedience. The Bible itself contains numerous examples of civil disobedience. The most prominent example of this is the confrontation between the kingdom of Jesus and the kingdom of Pilate on Easter morning, when God ordered his angel to break Pilate's seal and strike down his guards. Wherever the work of the Liberator is opposed, it is up to the Christian community to follow this example and the example of the apostles who declared, "We must obey God rather than human beings."

The key question for urban issues then becomes, "In what sectors of our cities is the work of the Liberator being challenged?" It is impossible to answer this question concretely without serious attention to what the Bible says about God's bias in favor of the widow, the orphan, the sojourner, the prisoner, and the beggar. In biblical times these were types of individuals who stood helpless and without legitimate voice before the structures of a patriarchal and ethnocentric society. Who are the helpless ones today?

When we have identified those helpless ones we need to think carefully and then act so that the result will be not mere individual charity (although that is in some instances appropriate) but rather the transformation of our entire social, economic, and political system to one more responsive to human needs. Our challenge is to effect this change sensitively, in harmony with the full range of divine norms which bear on human life: the responsible uses of natural and human resources, concern for the rebellious and the broken, and love for truth and mercy. If we persevere, the full good news of God's creating and redeeming love may touch the deepest life of the city.

AN ANABAPTIST THEOLOGICAL PERSPECTIVE ON ECONOMIC GROWTH

Dwight J. McFadden, Jr., training specialist,
Victor S. Weaver, Inc.

Economics, according to English economist Alfred Marshall (*Principles of Economics,* 1890), is the study of individuals and societies in the ordinary business of getting and using material goods.

The significance of economic activity is underscored by Marshall's observation that:

> Religious motives are more intense than economic, but their direct action seldom extends over so large a part of life. For the business by which a person earns his livelihood generally fills his thoughts during by far the greater part of those hours when his mind is at its best; during them his character is being formed by the way in which he uses his faculties in his work, by the thoughts and the feelings which they suggest, and by his relations to his associates in work, his employers or his employees.

To suggest (as our title might) that Anabaptists, past or present, have or had a formal theological consensus on economics or economic growth is probably somewhat misleading. Historically, Anabaptists considered themselves not so much theologians as Biblicists, or believers whose main concern was to recreate an authentic New Testament community in the world. To define this community, Anabaptists developed corporate articles of faith which included guidelines for day-to-day life, both for individuals and for the community as a whole. It is thus in this more general and practical sense that we can speak of an Anabaptist theological perspective on economics.

At this point a little historical background might be helpful. Anabaptists came into being as part of the original Reformed movement of the 1500s. Anabaptist leaders enlarged on the teaching of Luther and Zwingli, developed their own doctrinal statements and articles of faith, and set out to achieve them in actual experience. They started by organizing a church, composed solely of earnest Christians. The Anabaptist vision included three key points: first, that the essence of Christianity is discipleship; second, that the essence of the church is mutual love; and third, that the bases of Christian ethics are love and nonresistance.

The word Anabaptist means rebaptized. The name was originally used by their religious enemies and persecutors because Anabaptists practiced believer's baptism in addition to their Catholic baptism as infants.

Despite (or perhaps because of) persecution, Anabaptist beliefs attracted many new followers. Unlike other Reformers, Anabaptists completely repudiated the Catholic Church. For this, they were persecuted by both the Catholic Church and by other Reformers, including Luther and Zwingli. Contemporary Mennonites and Hutterites in the United States and Canada trace their roots to these early Anabaptists.

The concept of economic growth may also need some introduction. For our purposes, economic growth can be defined as the expansion over a period of years of an economy's capacity to produce real goods and services. It is sometimes helpful to think in terms of an analogy between economic growth and biological growth. Biological growth is a process by which material is introduced into the organism and transferred from one part of it to another so that the organism expands. Economic growth involves similar processes in an economic organism. In the context of this discussion, the economic organism is the entire complex of people, factories, stores, farms, rivers, dams, banks, and underlying ideas that produce the nation's yearly output of goods and services.

The key questions are: what forces determine the growth of this economic organism, and to what extent can they be altered?

One theory is that economic growth is the result of interplay between cultural forces and economic productivity. These cultural forces include science, technology, population changes, religion, and politics, and also social attitudes toward work, material possessions, and so on. The rate of economic productivity determines the amount of money left over, after expenses and taxes, to invest in goods-producing or capital equipment.

These cultural and economic forces converge when investment occurs; this is the embryonic moment for economic growth. In order to have funds to invest, individuals, businesses, and the economy as a whole must avoid spending all current resources. This is the act of saving. Investment then translates these savings into productive equipment and technology, and causes the economy to grow.

To measure this growth the government uses an indicator called the Gross National Product (GNP). The GNP monitors the level of current production by showing the total value of all goods and services produced by the economy as a whole over a given time period, usually one year.

GNP is measured in two different ways; either as the money spent to buy these goods and services or as the money received for producing them. The first measure is called the flow-of-product method; the second is known as the earnings-and-loss method. Theoretically the two should always be equal. A dollar spent by consumers equals a dollar received by producers which is then either applied to business expenses or taxes or retained as profit.

In computing GNP, economists count only the production of those goods and services that actually reach the consumer. For instance, GNP would include only the value of the packaged loaves of bread consumers bring home from the supermarket, not the gross receipts of the farmer who grew the wheat, the millers, the shippers, the packagers, the advertisers, the wholesalers, and everyone else involved in producing the final loaves of bread.

The final value of the bread equals the value added by these intermediaries.

Economic growth has been the object of much controversy in recent years. Today there is much concern about how such growth is consuming irreplaceable resources and causing environmental pollution. But at one time it was almost axiomatic that unlimited economic growth was both desirable and attainable. Many government and industry leaders still seem to hold to these beliefs. According to these proponents, such growth is the best way to maintain our advantage in international relations and to provide for defense needs. Many critics find this policy dangerously militaristic. Another argument advanced by growth advocates suggests that economic growth helps to prevent social strife. They claim that economic expansion not only keeps employment levels high and thus gives the employed a stake in continuing prosperity, but that it also makes possible the steady stream of goods and services that people need and want. As long as everyone is receiving a bigger piece of a bigger pie, there seems to be a tendency, in the short run, to be satisfied. This is so even if the piece allotted to the poor is a constant or decreasing share of the total.

Experience shows that growth does not eliminate social strife. The phenomenon is far too complex to have a single cause. Nonetheless, economic expansionists like to suggest that more and better products and services solve more problems. As they see it, each year growth leads to a better life for all of society, with benefits such as higher quality health care for the poor, better mass transportation, more urban renewal, and even improvements in environmental protection. However, as we now know, recent high technology has actually caused many of the problems for which newer products must compensate, while pollution is causing serious and possibly irremediable health and environmental damage.

Because the nation is now experiencing so many acute side effects of reckless expansion—environmental pollution, dwindling resources, and economic disparity—it may be tempting to see economic growth per se as the root of the problem. This would seem to miss the point that economic growth, as much as physical or spiritual growth, is a sign of life and health. The more relevant question is not whether economic growth should be supported, but what kinds of growth should be encouraged and in what sectors.

It is at this point that Anabaptists have something to say about the current nature of economic growth, and about some possible options to the pattern. To begin, we can look briefly at five of the twenty articles of the Mennonite Confession of Faith, and suggest how Anabaptists might apply these doctrines and principles to the issues of economic growth.

> 1) *God's creation and providence.* In the beginning God created all things by His Son; all existence is therefore finite and dependent upon Him. God created human beings in His own image, so that in free will, moral character, superior intellect, and spiritual nature, they resemble their Creator.
>
> In His providence, God is concerned with the lives of all His children, and in everything works for their eternal good. He has endowed human beings with the power of self-determination, and holds them responsible for their moral choices.

Because Anabaptists believe that God created everything, most would agree that he deliberately allows those choices and talents which can lead to economic and technological growth. At the same time, they would expect humans to be accountable for those choices. If we grant that self-determination and superior intellect are best used to provide for personal well-being and the well-being of society at large, it follows that Anabaptists will not engage in activities that might cheat or impoverish fellow humans, or that might despoil the environment.

2) *The Church of Christ.* The church of Christ is defined by its nature, function, and discipline. The church is a fellowship of believers whose membership is voluntary upon response to God's offer of salvation in Christ. Spirit-led conferences assist local congregations in maintaining biblical standards of faith, conduct, stewardship, and missions.

The task of the church is to demonstrate to the world the will of God, to witness to the saving power and intention of God in Christ, and to make disciples of all nations.

The church is to function as a family, in which each one is concerned for the spiritual and material welfare of other members. This concern extends to restore those in error, to assist those in need of finances or encouragement, and to willingly give and receive counsel.

The purposes of discipline are to lead each member to full stature in Christ, to restore to full fellowship the members who fall into sin, to clarify for all members the meaning of Christian discipleship, to promote the purity of the church, and to maintain the good name and witness of the church before the world.

From these statements we can see that Anabaptists expect believers to lead lives of love and discipline, and to maintain biblical standards of faith, conduct, stewardship, and mission. These individual ethics would seem to apply just as fully in the larger marketplace or at the corporate level in the production of goods and services. While it is possible to increase profits by exploiting various factors of production (formerly, labor, capital, land, management; now, energy, technology, capital), Anabaptists would want to consider what effects such practices would have on the intended witness of the church, and on personal relationships both within and outside the fellowship.

This second article also suggests that Anabaptists are to aid one another rather than seek the advantage. The provision for giving and receiving counsel could help correct and restore those whose business actions do not meet this standard.

3) *The Mission of the Church to Society.* Christ has commissioned the church to make disciples of all the nations, baptizing them and teaching them to observe His commandment. While He was on earth, Jesus Himself fed the hungry, healed the sick, and had compassion on the poor. The church should likewise minister to all those who are in physical or social need and to those who are physically or emotionally ill. The church should witness against racial discrimination, economic injustice, and all forms of human slavery and moral degradation.

This article introduces a universal theme to the ministry of the church, both in terms of the scope of appropriate activities, and in international outlook. It also specifically directs Anabaptists to oppose economic injustice. These two statements suggest how Anabaptists might respond to multinational corporate growth that exploits the world's less developed countries. This international consciousness might also translate into a personal decision to cut consumption of goods that are produced at the expense of economic and technological progress in the Third World.

> 4) *Discipleship and Nonconformity.* Christ and Satan are the heads of two opposing kingdoms to which humans give spiritual allegiance. The kingdom of Christ consists of the born again, who manifest only love toward those of other races, cultures, and economic levels. Because they regard their bodies as temples of the Holy Spirit, believers will consider their best adornment to be a beauty of the Spirit, expressed in attire that is modest, economical, simple, and becoming. Christians should seek to be faithful in their stewardship of money and possessions.

Anabaptists might use this tenet to question whether their economic decisions are fundamentally different from those of the world. Because each purchase encourages growth in a particular industry or sector, Anabaptists may want to reconsider the kinds of goods and services their spending actually supports.

Love and stewardship are also key in this article. Anabaptists might want to think about what changes these ethics suggest for an economic system whose chief principle of growth (supply and demand) generates recurring conditions (inflation and recession) that invariably discriminate against the poor.

> 5) *Love and Nonresistance.* God wants His children to follow Christian love in all human relationships. The supreme model for such a life of love excluding all retaliation and revenge is Jesus Himself. Christians are to avoid reprisal in every area of life: in personal injustice, in situations where people commonly resort to litigation, in industrial strife, and in international tensions and war. Nonresistant Christians will neither serve in any office which employs the use of force, nor will they participate in military service, or training, or in the voluntary financial support of war. Nevertheless at the risk of life itself, Christians must do whatever they can to alleviate human distress and suffering.

This statement of faith is based on a love ethic which affirms the supreme worth of all individuals. For Anabaptists it would seem to enjoin any economic activity or policy that compromises the health, financial security, or living conditions of any person or group, either now or in the future.

Traditionally, Anabaptists have avoided organized conflict. For these believers, the antithesis of nonresistance is militarism in any form: military training and service, armament production, and defense contracts and research. This ethic tends to undercut any argument that make defense spending a significant factor in economic growth. Because of this bias, many Anabaptists divert their military tax allotment to relief efforts. Ideally, at the last resort, Anabaptists would risk life itself to alleviate human suffering caused by economic injustice.

Because they are principles of faith, rather than technical statements, these five articles will not supply detailed guidelines for economic change. Even if they did, such solutions would be quickly outdated in today's fast-paced marketplace. However, seen as functional requirements for an economy based on justice and love, these principles allow Anabaptists of any period to appraise contemporary economic policies, and to design new economic programs appropriate to that setting. This, in fact, describes what Anabaptists have traditionally done and are still doing through their associations for mutual aid.

MUTUAL AID AND ECONOMIC GROWTH

The paramount theme of early Anabaptist history was, "Bear ye one another's burdens and so fulfill the law of Christ." In times of need, these first Anabaptists helped not only each other but also those outside the fellowship.

When persecution by the established church forced Anabaptists from the cities, they relocated to rural areas where they attracted more converts. Many Anabaptists fled to other countries where they were offered shelter and religious freedom. Those who went to Russia and Prussia divided equal shares of land so that each parcel had the same amount of good and bad acreage. When a couple married, families assigned them a section of land and helped to furnish the new home.

These early Anabaptists also established trust funds for widows and orphans which grew into organizations that resemble our contemporary banks. Mutual aid societies insured against property damage and set up mutual stock breeding programs to improve local herds. Life was based on cooperation, rather than competition. Latter-day mutual aid programs are modeled after these early associations.

The Mennonite Mutual Aid Association was originally founded in 1945 to provide jobs, housing loans, and insurance for men returning home from alternate military service, and to offer job training for rural youth who wanted to work in the cities. Today the association continues to add new services. A recent innovation is a loan program to help pastors secure housing down payments.

A service organization with a different thrust began in 1953, when a group of businessmen created the Mennonite Economic Development Association. Initially most of their work was overseas, helping to start small businesses in economically strained areas. More recently this group is performing a similar function in the United States. Under the Mennonite Central Committee relief agency, a consultant from this group offers business counseling and economic assistance to small businesses in the city as part of an urban ministries outreach.

A third Mennonite mutual aid program, Jeff-Von-Lou, grew out of the efforts of a local congregation some years ago. Since that time, it has worked to build community solidarity by meeting local needs. Under the leadership of Macler Shepard, this action group managed a housing redevelopment project that provided jobs and housing in the community. It has successfully recruited businesses like the Brown Shoe Company by developing formal community marketing plans to analyze available labor pools, revenue potential, and economic stability. Other projects include a youth leadership program, child-care centers, and committee work on school and political boards.

Future economic conditions may suggest different needs such as community centers or food cooperatives for direct relief; more consulting services for small business development; skills training for service oriented jobs; or organized efforts to reduce energy consumption, environmental pollution, and production of nonessential goods and services.

The three preceding mutual aid programs demonstrate that economic growth need not necessarily take place at the expense of the poor. Growth based on the principles of justice and love can benefit workers, management, and community alike. This kind of witness is both a sign and a foretaste of the kingdom of God.

EVANGELIZATION AND RENEWAL

EVANGELIZING AN AWAKENING GIANT: HISPANICS IN THE U.S.

Orlando E. Costas, professor, Eastern Baptist Theological Seminary

"Enough! You can no longer ignore us!"

With these shouts, a group of Hispanic Protestant leaders interrupted New York's 1981 Riverside Church National Conference on the City to deliver a statement in which they charged that:

1) Social issues relevant to the Hispanic community—undocumented aliens, U.S. foreign policy in Latin America, the impact of multinational corporations in Latin America, bilingual education in America, and the adverse impact of Reagan's economics on the Hispanic people—are not given significant attention in the conferences and media programs funded and staffed by the North American religious establishment.

2) Contributions of Hispanic people in the life and ministry of the church in the city are systematically and categorically ignored. National and regional conferences, (such as the Riverside Church Conference on the City, Washington 1980, and the American Festival on Evangelism) exclude significant participation of indigenous Hispanics both in planning and in implementation. The absence of Hispanic speakers in regional and national events deprives the Christian community of vital Hispanic perspectives.

3) The North American religious establishment must assume its share of responsibility for urban decay and for the deplorable conditions under which many Hispanics must live in U.S. cities. The church's policy in Hispanic communities has been to neglect, desert, or undermine the resources of the Hispanic people. The only churches that have remained to serve the spiritual needs of Hispanic peoples in inner cities are indigenous and independent Hispanic churches.

4) Hispanic liturgy and theology have been denied their rightful place in the North American religious community. Our music, theology, literature, and language have been rejected. The church has served as an instrument of assimilation instead of human liberation and fulfillment. The church has perpetuated paternalism, division, and oppression which have mitigated against the development of and deprived the North American religious establishment of the contributions of Hispanic religious experience.

5) Theological seminaries and graduate schools of religion have discriminated against Hispanics by refusing to hire indigenous Hispanic faculty, provide supportive services, or allocate financial resources. The

55

educational establishment has rejected the legitimacy of bilingual theological education as a viable and indispensable ingredient for men and women for ministry.

In conclusion, the group demanded, first, "immediate and complete responses to these serious complaints and indictments to the American religious establishment; and second, the funding of a conference that would bring together the Hispanic leadership of the church in North America and Puerto Rico."

The conference was stunned at this unexpected demonstration. Conference planners offered public apologies, and that evening an offering was raised to help Hispanic leaders plan the consultation they demanded.

This episode illustrates only too well both the tragic and explosive reality of Hispanics in the United States, and the seeming indifference of the North American church. Even though Riverside Church is located in a Hispanic neighborhood, and even though New York City has more than 500 Spanish-speaking churches and one of the largest Hispanic populations in the country, it did not occur to conference planners to incorporate the concerns and the leadership of the urban Hispanic church into their agenda. If here, of all places, it took a dramatic and forceful upset for Hispanics to get any kind of recognition, one can only wonder what action might be required to gain the attention of the mainstream church and society as a whole.

The issue is very serious indeed. Hispanics represent one of the fastest growing ethnic groups in the United States. Twenty-five years ago, there were some 5 million Hispanics in North America; by 1981, the official number was 15 million, with an unofficial estimate of more than 23 million. This translates to a growth rate of 2.2 percent per annum. The sheer size of this ethnic bloc would seem reason for North American society in general, and the mainstream church in particular, to make Hispanics a top priority for the 1980s. But in point of fact, we observe no such interest. Instead, both the North American church and society at large appear unconcerned and uninformed about the Hispanic community.

Our purpose here is to offer some background about the Hispanic community in the United States and about the challenges it is beginning to pose to the North American church and to society; and beyond that, to suggest several factors both within and outside the Hispanic community that may affect its readiness to hear and respond to the Gospel.

THE REALITY OF HISPANICS IN THE UNITED STATES

Hispanics in North America can generally be grouped into four major categories according to their patterns of immigration. In the first group are the early settlers of the Southwest (Texas, Colorado, Arizona, California, and New Mexico), on hand many years before the arrival of Anglo-Americans (mainly from the North American South) and northern Europeans (mostly from Germany). Some of these Hispanic families go back to the very first Spanish settlers. By now, members of this group hardly consider themselves foreigners. From their perspective, Anglos (a term coined by Mexican Americans to describe all those of European descent) are the newcomers. The signs of these early settlers are everywhere—in our architecture, in the names of our towns, cities, and streets, and in our language and culture.

Hispanics in the second group, the established immigrants, began to emigrate from Mexico, Puerto Rico, and Cuba early in the twentieth century. They were preceded by the sixteenth- and early nineteenth-century Hispanic settlers of St. Augustine and Tampa, Florida, and by a later influx of Cubans attracted to the tobacco industry in Ybor City, Tampa's Latin quarter. (Interestingly enough, José Martí, the well-known Cuban leader, traveled there to enlist recruits for Cuba's war of independence.)

The majority of these established immigrants, however, arrived after World War II, in the later 1940s, 1950s, and 1960s. By now they are settled and have jobs. Their children either came with them when they were very young or were born here. Many of them have retained their former language and culture, but on the whole they have all learned to survive (and in some cases to succeed) in Anglo-American culture.

A third group includes the new immigrants of the 1970s and 1980s. Among them are Mexicans that by the millions are streaming over the 2,000-mile border from unauthorized points of entry. Also included in this group are thousands of Dominicans who fled to the United States between 1965 and 1966 after the Dominican Republic's civil war, and an even larger wave from that country in the 1970s. In 1980, they were joined by more than 100,000 Cubans. Over the past several years economic, political, and military upheaval in Central America has also added growing numbers of Guatemalans, Salvadorans, and Nicaraguans to this group, until Salvadorans alone now number more than 500,000. Last among these new immigrants are significant enclaves of Chileans, Argentinians, Colombians, and other ethnic groups from Spanish South America, and even some sprawling Brazilian contingencies (though not as many, and they, of course, speak Portuguese).

The last group of Hispanics is the new generation, the children of the established immigrants. They are usually bilingual, although some speak only English. They still eat traditional food and are generally Hispanic in their approach to life, but their first language is either English or "Spanglish" (a mixture of English and Spanish). In most cases, they do not feel at ease in Anglo society. They are the Galileans, looked down on by both Latin Americans for their cultural impurity, and by Anglos for their ethnic ties.

Because each of these four groups is unique in background and experience, each one tends to have its own problems, its own attitudes toward contemporary North American society, and its own preferred lifestyle.

Hispanics are concentrated in several regions of the country. The largest and most densely populated area, because of its direct historical ties with Spain, is the Southwest. States such as Texas, Arizona, New Mexico, and California, together with parts of Colorado, have a strong Hispanic cultural tradition. Today they represent the largest Hispanic contingent in the United States. In terms of total Hispanic population, Texas, with its 3 million Hispanics, and New Mexico, where Spanish is as common as English, are second only to California. Projections for that state now indicate that more than 50 percent of its total population will be Spanish-speaking or of

Spanish descent by the end of the decade.

The second largest Hispanic settlement is located in the Northeast, with New York City as its hub. Distribution ranges as far north as the New Hampshire—Massachusetts border and as far south as Washington, D.C. The greater New York metropolitan area has at least 2 million Hispanics, New Jersey nearly 500, 000, and Connecticut and Pennsylvania more than 200,000 each. Hispanics tend to be a social, cultural, and political force throughout this region.

In the Midwest, Chicago is the center of the third most densely populated region. Its one million Hispanics represent every major Spanish-speaking nationality. There are also large numbers of Hispanics in the industrial cities of Ohio, Michigan, Indiana, and Wisconsin, and small pockets in Iowa, Missouri, and Kansas.

The fourth region, center of two distinct Hispanic populations, is the Southeast. St. Augustine, the oldest city in the country, is also one of the nation's oldest Hispanic settlements. But Dade County, Florida, is by far the youngest and fastest growing Hispanic community in the United States, as the result of a massive Cuban influx over the last two decades. Since 1970, central Florida has also experienced a steady gain of Hispanic immigrants from the Midwest and the Southeast. Major southern cities like Atlanta and New Orleans (the latter a traditional port of entry for many Central Americans) are also seeing an increase in their Hispanic populations. If current trends hold, the Southeast will continue to expand as a major Hispanic center for many years to come, both because of movement south to the Sun Belt, and because of growing migration from the Caribbean basin.

The smallest region, but another site of rapid growth, is the Pacific Northwest. Rural sectors of eastern Washington, Idaho, and Oregon now house large concentrations of Hispanic farm workers, but most of these Hispanics will probably relocate to major cities such as Seattle and Portland within the next decade.

On the whole, Hispanics in all five of these regions are poor and getting poorer. In 1980, the median family income in the United States for a family of four was $17,640; among Hispanics it was $12,566. When that figure is broken down, an even greater disparity becomes evident: the median family income of Mexicans was $10,500; of Cubans, $15,326; and of Puerto Ricans, $8,282. Thus, while the Hispanic community taken as a whole would be slightly better off than its black neighbors (who had a family income of $10,874), when one compares black income with the two largest groups of Hispanics in the United States, Mexicans and Puerto Ricans, Mexicans earn slightly less than blacks, and Puerto Ricans the least of all.

The same relative order appears in the unemployment rate. Toward the end of 1980, nationwide employment stood at 6.6 percent. Yet, the unemployment rate among Mexicans was 10.6 percent; among Cubans, 11.6 percent (largely due to increased numbers of new refugees); among blacks, 15 percent; and among Puerto Ricans, 15.5 percent.

Probably the key factor in this chronic unemployment is that 70 percent of Hispanics are unskilled. If they can find work at all, Hispanics generally hold the lowest paying blue collar and farm jobs. As a result, the Hispanic community tends to have the largest number of people living at or below the poverty level. While in 1980, 9.3 percent of all families in the United States were classified as poverty level, for Hispanics as a whole the rate was 21.4 percent, and for Puerto Ricans, 38.9 percent.

Hispanics are not only poor; worse yet, they are becoming key constituents in the growing permanent under-class that now inhabits the nation's major industrial cities. On the one hand this under-class is made up of drug pushers and drug addicts, prostitutes, muggers, welfare defrauders, and the chronically unemployed. They are the expendables, the social outcasts, economic and political nonpersons. On the other hand, it also includes the Hispanic poor who find themselves trapped in these ghetto underworlds in a growing number of economically depressed North American cities.

Despite their poverty, their diverse origins, and their scattered distribution across the country, Hispanics in the United States are a distinct cultural unit with a common cultural root. North American Hispanic life takes its special flavor first from several centuries of contact with Africa both in the Iberian peninsula and in the Americas, and second (and perhaps more importantly) from the intermingling of Iberian and Amerind cultures in the New World. Little wonder that the Mexican philosopher José Basconcelos described the people of Latin America as the "cosmic race," fruit of the convergence of three civilizations (African, Aboriginal, and European). This historical and cultural blend is unique to Hispanics who are thus distinguished not only by their common language, but also by their common anthropological experience.

For the majority of Hispanics in the United States, the Spanish language is the bond that reinforces this cultural unity. To the Anglo world they are collectively known as "Spanish-speaking peoples," and Hispanics themselves see Spanish as the chief source of their composite social identity. For this reason, bilingualism is becoming as crucial an issue for Hispanics as public integration has been for blacks and other nonwhite minorities.

Hispanics in the United States also share a singular Catholic religiocultural background derived from Iberian Catholicism and its historical encounters with African and aboriginal religions. Nearly a millennium of confrontation with Islam and Judaism, culminating in the Inquisition, left Iberian Catholicism intolerant and aggressive. Fearful of syncretism in the New World, the Iberian church forced European cultural and religious patterns on its indigenous converts.

In time, these aboriginal, African, and *mestizo* (mixed) populations incorporated many of their former customs and beliefs into their new faith. In this sense, Latin American Christendom is a new phenomenon, differing in form and content not only from the Catholicism of western and eastern Europe, but also from that of the Iberian peninsula.

Throughout the colonial period in Latin America, the ecclesiastical hierarchy functioned as an arm of the state, but during the first century of independence the church lost ground with the new ruling elite. Nevertheless, cultural Catholicism became deeply ingrained in the popular folkways, finding expression in colorful fiestas and religious holidays, and in elaborate rites and ceremonies. It is in this sense, and generally not as a transforming personal faith, that Christianity is understood and practiced by most Hispanics today.

Another characteristic of the Hispanic community is its strong sense of family. Like Semitic and other ethnic groups, Hispanics tend to see large families both as a guarantee of prosperity for the immediate future, and as a source of security for old age. This pattern is common to both rural and urban dwellers.

Hispanics today find themselves gaining in political stature, if for no other reason than sheer numbers. Despite a history of political oppression (the Southwest is a conquered territory, Puerto Rico an occupied island, and the Caribbean and Central America to this day de facto colonies), their story now is one of emerging electoral power. The older established generation long ago laid a political base in Texas, New Mexico, southern California, and New York City. As a result, Hispanics have traditionally elected a small number of representatives from these districts and also one or two senators from New Mexico. But as politicians have become increasingly aware of the growing number of eligible Hispanic voters both political parties have begun to court their favor in state and national elections, and a growing number of political organizations now lobby for Hispanic candidates and issues.

From this brief overview, it is probably apparent that the Hispanic population in the United States is indeed a giant, both in terms of its strength of numbers and of its enormous problems. But the Hispanic population is also an awakening giant, that is, its challenges to the North American church and to society have only recently begun to surface. The effects of this stirring can be seen in four important areas.

THE CHALLENGE OF HISPANICS

First, Hispanics are beginning to undermine the provincialism of mainstream North American society. In a world where most other nations conduct their affairs in two, three, or four different tongues, the United States is still essentially monolingual. The average North American tends to think of English as a universal language, and even academics are scarcely less narrow-minded. As one college professor remarked, "Foreign languages? That's not important any more. Because if anything is worthy of publication, it will wind up in four major languages: German, Russian, French, or English. So long as you know one of these, you are all set!" Nevertheless, in the Americas alone, more than one half of the people speak Spanish or Portuguese, not English, and Spanish now ranks fourth among the world's most spoken languages.

Formerly it was only as Anglos began to travel that they became aware of their linguistic deficiencies. As a bilingual community, Hispanics now challenge that monolingualism at home. Indeed, they may eventually challenge the primacy of English itself in North America, because they represent an American language bloc that will, by the turn of the century, be more than 600 million strong.

Second, Hispanics now challenge North American society over a broad range of both urban and rural issues. Their presence has intensified social, economic, and political pressures in each of these two sectors. For example, many of the nation's farm workers are now undocumented Hispanic aliens. Many small farmers depend on these Hispanic laborers despite their illegal status because they are readily available, hard working, and willing to accept low wages. These workers increase tensions between enforcement agencies, farmers, and other domestic farm labor. A different kind of pressure has been brought to bear by César Chávez, whose United Farm Workers' Organizing Committee (UFWOC), revolutionized the social and economic structure of agriculture in California. Inspired by these efforts, resident Hispanics and other farm workers all over the country are now forming similar bargaining units. While union gains are being undercut by farmers who continue to hire undocumented aliens, in recent years there has been some attempt to organize this latter group also.

In New Mexico, Hispanics have challenged the federal government through an organization called the Federal Alliance of Land Grants, in a militant struggle for the recovery of land awarded to early Hispanic settlers by the kings of Spain. Initiated in the early 1960s under the leadership of former Pentecostal pastor Reies López Tijerina, the Alianza (as it is popularly known) has sought to regain millions of acres of grant lands originally guaranteed to Mexican Americans by the Treaty of Guadalupe Hidalgo (1849). The Alianza has not only launched a series of law suits to reclaim this territory, but has also proposed the creation of a Confederation of Free City-States in rural New Mexico. Needless to say, the case is generating great interest in New Mexico and throughout most of the Southwest.

Hispanics are also key figures in North American cities. On the one hand, because of their enormous social, cultural, economic, and religious deprivation, they strain every major urban system. On the other, Hispanics are also among community leaders helping to organize city neighborhoods socially, economically, and politically. (Strong cultural and religious organizations have always been characteristic of urban Hispanics.) Hispanics are now beginning to demand an increasing share of city resources through direct participation in city decision making. Thus Hispanics are adding not only their concerns and problems, but also their talents to overcrowded urban agendas.

Third, Hispanics are becoming increasingly identified with long-standing problems in international relations. The example closest to home is their role in United States-Mexican relations. Mexican resources have always held great attraction for the United States. One need only recall that Texas and the Southwest were originally annexed from Mexico to appreciate the extent of this appeal. Given the energy crisis of the last several years, Mexican reserves, this time in the form of oil and uranium deposits, are once more in demand by the United States. Despite this ready North American market, however, access to these resources will largely depend on how the United States responds to its growing numbers of Hispanic undocumented aliens. With millions out of work in Mexico, current United States policies of legal sanctions, prosecution, and deportation are not likely to improve trade relations between the two countries.

A second area of long-term diplomatic concern is the Caribbean. One reason (though by no means the only one) that relations between Cuba and the United States have not improved is that farmers in the south, especially in Florida, have lobbied strongly against this course. In this way, they protect southern agribusiness from direct competition with Cuba's highly centralized and socialized economy and its lower paid labor force. Another chronic United States-Cuban sore point is the steady stream of Cuban political and economic refugees into the United States. Over the years, the United States has offered political asylum to well over 100,000 Cubans, a gesture that has also had serious economic and social repercussions in this nation.

In much the same way, our past history of involvement in Central American countries such as Nicaragua, El Salvador, and Guatemala is now bearing fruit in the present tremendous influx of undocumented migrants from these countries. Even the supposedly domestic question of the future status of Puerto Rico has been hotly debated in the United Nations' Committee on Decolonization for more than ten years. Thus Hispanics in the United States are also a community of international significance.

Finally, Hispanics are beginning to challenge the North American church as a foreign mission field inside the United States. For many years Latin America has been a focus of intense evangelistic concern. One third of all Protestant missionaries and one half of the Catholic missionary force from both the United States and Canada are now concentrated in Latin America. One can well understand the ecclesiastical attraction of a mission field that offers churches growing by leaps and bounds, an admirable number of martyrs, and a vibrant and courageous theology.

However, the same Christians who willingly invest in Latin American missions are apparently unaware that Hispanics in the United States comprise the fourth largest Spanish-speaking population in the world. The North American church has yet to acknowledge this internal Hispanic nation or to consider its unique spiritual needs.

THE EVANGELISTIC PROSPECTS OF HISPANICS

Perhaps a first step in meeting this last challenge would be to recognize that there are specific factors within the Hispanic community that may either advance or obstruct the spread of the Gospel.

On the positive side, Hispanics in the United States tend to be a people in search of meaning. As migrants uprooted from homelands, relatives, and friends, they often abandon traditional cultural and spiritual values so that important parts of their identity become blurred. A strong faith would help them to survive and live productive lives in an alien environment. Most Hispanics appear not only open but eager for a message that will restore their self-image, make sense of their migrant existence, and offer hope for a better life.

The receptivity of Hispanics to the Gospel is also enhanced by their familiarity with the symbols of the Christian faith. Unlike Asians and Africans who are generally religiously distant from Christianity, most Hispanics are not complete strangers to the language of the Gospel. And unlike Anglo-Americans and Europeans who have been swayed by the Enlightenment,

Hispanics do not often labor over the dispute between reason and faith. Intellectual atheism and secular humanism are not, for the most part, Hispanic issues. But while Hispanics can, in general, accept the claims of the Christian faith and identify with its symbols, they may have difficulty with the concept that the Gospel is not just a story from the past, but a personal spiritual reality with implications for their economic, social, and political welfare.

The prospects for evangelism are also furthered by several Hispanic cultural traits: their common language, their strong sense of family, and their communities of national origin. All of these relationships represent natural bridges for contact and communication. These ties not only encourage personal exchange of the Gospel, but the latter two also provide a healthy setting for growth in the faith.

Another favorable sign is the presence of vigorous Spanish-speaking churches in every major Hispanic neighborhood. These churches have generally gone unnoticed by mainstream Christianity, perhaps because many of them meet in storefronts or in other settings as unlikely as old theaters, former synagogues and temples, and assorted commercial buildings. Inside, however, one finds enthusiastic communities of faith, bearing vibrant witness for Jesus Christ and nurturing those who come to faith.

One last point in their favor is the large number of unused Anglo church facilities in the inner city. As Hispanics have moved into major urban centers, many Anglo churches have either collapsed or experienced dramatic drops in membership. Some of these facilities could be invaluable to new Hispanic congregations in their efforts to evangelize the Hispanic community.

THE OBSTACLES TO HISPANIC EVANGELISM

From a negative point of view, one of the key obstacles to Hispanic evangelism is the Anglo church itself. In the past, most Anglo churches and Christian organizations simply ignored the whole question of mission to Hispanics and concentrated instead on Latin America. More recently, many Anglo congregations and denominations in the inner city have been too preoccupied with their own survival to consider the needs of their Hispanic neighbors. Attempts at joint ministry to the Hispanic community have been frustrated by social tensions between North American and Hispanic congregations. Hispanic churches that might otherwise grow are often limited by a lack of funds and inadequate meeting space. Anglo congregations leaving the inner city often compound this problem by listing church properties on the open market, rather than negotiating with Hispanic churches to ensure a continuity of Christian witness in urban neighborhoods.

Thus, the majority of mainline and evangelical denominations not only fail in direct support to Hispanic evangelism, but they also often undermine struggling Hispanic congregations. The investment of evangelical outreach ministries in the Hispanic community has been so recent and so tentative as to be almost negligible.

Two other major obstacles to Hispanic evangelism occur within the Hispanic church itself. One of the most devastating is that of Christendom, or cultural Christianity, a chronic problem for many church communities in the Western world. This Christendom is not the sum total of Christians in the world; it is, rather, a world view that equates Western culture with Christian society so that any given political system is assumed to be based on Christian principles and values and to have the church as its manager or mentor. The history of Christianity in the Hispanic world has been one of successive Christendoms, each characterized by the mass observance of Christianity and by the absence of serious discipleship. What one finds in the Hispanic world is a tendency toward mass evangelism with little concern for either the content of the message or the quality of the response. As a result the Hispanic church on the whole is deficient both in terms of its own spiritual growth, and in its role as an agent of justice, freedom, and peace. Once again, mass culture and Christianity have become almost synonymous. Christendom in this sense is a menace to evangelism and it is rampant in the Hispanic community. Hispanics need to hear that the Gospel liberates believers to transform the world for good.

Besides Christendom, one last stumbling block to evangelism is the misconception within the Hispanic church that the work of sharing the Gospel properly belongs to a few highly visible professional evangelists, or to the clergy, rather than to the congregation and to the community. The Hispanic church has adopted a model of evangelism based on elaborate crusades and revival meetings that tend to reduce the entire role of the congregation to that of spectators at a sophisticated show.

These mass strategies are almost always counterproductive, first, because they are imposed from outside the congregation, and second, because they rarely produce lasting results.

For all the decisions for salvation and baptisms such programs may generate, time reveals all too few changed lives, committed congregations, or transformed institutions. But the point here is not so much that the meetings themselves are worthless (God, after all, can work in all places), but rather that any evangelistic undertaking on any scale needs to grow out of the continued concern, commitment, and most of all participation of the entire church body. Ultimately, the congregation is the best point of contact between the cultural and social reality of the people and the truth of the Gospel.

If there is to be authentic evangelism in the Hispanic community, urban church workers need to equip grassroots Christians first by teaching them to develop strategies that have *meaning* for *them*, and then by helping them to gain the skills and confidence to carry out those strategies. In this way, evangelism may grow out of its own accord, touching individual lives until the entire Hispanic community is transformed.

A CASE STUDY IN BLACK CHURCH RENEWAL

Jeremiah A. Wright, Jr., pastor,
Trinity United Church of Christ

The city of Chicago has long been recognized as one of the nation's citadels of great black clergy and congregations in the twentieth century. Alan Spears's *Black Chicago,* and Carter G. Woodson's *The History of the Negro Church* are but two of the many works to cite the tremendous ministries carried on in this city before 1970 by such well-known church leaders as the Reverends L.K. Williams, Reverdy Ransom, Joseph H. Jackson, Louis Boddie, Joseph Evans, Mary Evans, Clarence H. Cobbs, J.C. Austin, Sr., and William A. Johnson; and also to point out the tremendous contributions made by churches such as Institutional A.M.E., Quinn Chapel A.M.E., Pilgrim Baptist, Olivet Baptist, Metropolitan Community, and St. John Church-Baptist, to name just a few.

Add to this impressive galaxy that Chicago is also home to Professor Thomas Dorsey (the father of gospel music), the Ward Sisters, the Roberta Martin Singers, and the Rev. James Cleveland, and one may begin to see why Chicago is one of the national headquarters of the black church and the black religious tradition.

Since the mid 1950s, however, powerful sociological forces have eroded Chicago's position as a mecca for black religion. One cannot really begin to discuss one example of black church renewal in this city without first looking at the effect these forces have had on what has been called black church decline.

WHY DECLINE?

The 1954 Supreme Court desegration decision opened the legal door to public integration, and sparked the Montgomery bus boycott, the beginning of the civil rights movement, and the black power/black conciousness/black self-determination renaissance. Each of these events had its effect on the black church tradition in Chicago in ways that have not yet been fully measured. Demographic shifts in Chicago's ethnic neighborhoods accompanied these moves towards integration. In the final analysis changes in racial attitudes here were only cosmetic. Still, when the walls of the heretofore prescribed ghetto did come tumbling down, blacks by the hundreds of thousands began to move east, west, and far south, thereby draining the great black churches of the congregations that had filled their pews Sunday after Sunday.

Many of these parishioners continued to commute back and forth to their home churches. However, because of a number of other factors related to the limited open housing phenomenon in Chicago, these parishioners were largely restricted to the older generation, a dying breed of churchgoers at least as far as the old traditional great churches were concerned.

One of these factors was the new availability of social and recreational outlets (other than the church) previously segregated or off limits to blacks. At one time blacks had been rigidly restricted to *one* basic geographical area in the city. Almost any black Chicagoan over forty years of age attended DuSable, Phillips, or Dunbar High Schools.

Another factor that contributed to the decline was a shift in the spiritual climate of the nation which spilled over into the new black communities. No longer were they self-contained closely-knit extended families shielded from the Euro-American faith crisis. The loss of prayer from the public schools, the effects of the Dr. Spock mentality upon black family child-rearing patterns (e.g., no more mandatory church and Sunday school attendance), and the ascendancy of television (and to a lesser extent, movies) to the thrones once occupied by God and the black church all undermined the chances that younger blacks would replenish the ranks of those who continued to commute to the churches of their childhoods.

Commuting itself became a factor in the decline. The programs (and the ministry) of many of these churches were no longer aimed at their parish communities. Instead, they were increasingly geared toward the old dues-paying remnant who no longer lived near their churches, but who still faithfully attended worship, week after week. Yet another factor in the decline was what Gayraud Wilmore, in *Black Religion and Black Radicalism,* calls "the deradicalization of the black church." Wilmore describes in painful detail just how the black church, once a bastion of black radicalism, social protest, and moral reform in the black community, went through a period of deradicalization as the immediate attractions of integration lured parishioners and congregational leaders away from their commitments to black liberation and justice.

It was about *this* particular stage of the black church that E. Franklin Frazier wrote in *The Negro Church in America,* and it was this "Negro church" stage that alienated and drove away many black descendants of Chicago's old-line parishioners. As C. Eric Lincoln pointed out in *The Black Church Since Frazier,* "The turbulent decade of the sixties witnessed the death of the Negro Church in North America."

Nothing happens in a vacuum. Along with the moves out of the old neighborhoods, the spiritual malaise of white North Americans (witness the death of God theologies), and the desertion of South Side churches by succeeding generations, there came the civil rights movement, the black awareness era, and the unrelenting impact of the Black Muslims, *headquartered* in Chicago.

In place of the now dead "Negro church," stands the offspring of the conflict between "conscienceless power" and "powerless conscience."

That offspring is the black church which is still going through an unbelievable and exhilarating period of renewal, growth, and ascendancy. From the 1960s onward there has arisen both in Chicago and throughout the nation a new galaxy of stars to equal, if not eclipse, those mentioned earlier. Though their styles are not those of their predecessors (one of the by-products of the newfound pride in black culture), their impact on the black church tradition is just as great if not greater.

The full extent of these new individual and combined ministries cannot yet be told as they are still making history. One cannot, however, undertake any discussion either of the twentieth-century black church movement (in Chicago or the nation) or of black church renewal without mentioning the significant contributions of the Reverends Clay Evans, Wilbur Daniel, Floyd Piper, Shelvin Hall, Bishop Louis H. Ford, Donald Parsons, Jasper Williams, Roscoe Cooper, T. Garrott Benjamin, Charles G. Adams, Henry Gregory, John Bryant, and Otis Moss. Some men and their ministries spanned both of these eras (especially outside of Chicago): the Reverends Gardner Taylor, Sandy Ray, Howard Thurman, and J.A. Wright, Sr.

Nor can one discuss black church renewal in Chicago and the nation without some reference to the churches themselves: Fellowship Baptist Church (6,000 members, 1,000 of them added to the rolls in 1979 alone), Antioch Baptist Church (5,000 members), Mt. Calvary Baptist Church (5,000 members), Hartford Avenue Baptist Church of Detroit, Second Christian Church in Indianapolis (4,000 members), Fifth Street Baptist Church in Richmond, Virginia, 19th Street Baptist Church of Washington, DC, Concord Avenue Baptist Church in New York (12,000 members), Bethel A.M.E. Church of Baltimore, (4,000 members), and Trinity United Church of Christ in Chicago, just to name a few.

Time and space considerations do not permit an exhaustive list of the clergy and congregations who fall within the new breed category of C. Eric Lincoln's *Black Church in America.* However, it would be presumptuous not to preface our remarks about *one* model of black church renewal without pointing out that there are many other models, some with far more impressive track records than this one.

To understand the model of renewal at Trinity United Church of Christ, it is helpful to look at six specific areas.

I. THEOLOGICAL RATIONALE

The theological rationale of Trinity United Church of Christ is based on three elements: the ministry of Jesus, the Great Commission (Matthew 28:19,20), and the words and ideas of the hymn, "Lift Him Up!"

The ministry of Jesus as perceived and understood at Trinity is one that involves him, and therefore his disciples, in the lives of the downtrodden, the oppressed, the outcast, and those whom the system has written off.

The Great Commission is familiar to all Christians and does not need repeating here. What may require some examination and perhaps exegesis are the words and ideas of "Lift Him Up!" The two verses that contain lines directly related to Trinity's theological position are:

67

How to reach the *masses, men of every birth*
for an answer Jesus gave the Key,
"And I, if I be lifted up from the earth,
I'll draw all men unto me!"

Oh, the *world is hungry for the living bread*
Lift the Savior up for men to see
Trust Him, and do not doubt His Word
      When he said:
"I'll draw all men unto Me!"

The two key ideas (italicized for emphasis) are perhaps somewhat out of keeping with the stereotypes generally associated with a *northern* black UCC congregation. Nevertheless, they are pivotal to an understanding of Trinity's theological rationale. These themes presume an a priori commitment to the masses that involves consciously cutting across class, caste, and socioeconomic levels. Trinity utterly abandons and rejects the notion of the middle class as the proper vineyard into which God has called the church to labor. A commitment to the masses (*not* the classes), and a strong belief that humanity is, indeed, hungry for the bread of life to "come down from heaven," dovetail with the first two elements to provide a theological platform for Trinity.

II. PHILOSOPHY OF MINISTRY

"Building on cultural strengths," a philosophy articulated by Dr. Frances Holliday of Trinity UCC, is the phrase that perhaps best describes its philosophy of ministry. It begins with a premise suggested by Dr. Gardner Taylor in *How Shall They Preach?* He states that in choosing a watchman (Ezekiel 33), the people chose a person "of their own coasts" (i.e., one who has sat where they sit, one who knows their fears, hopes, joys, pain, and sorrows). It is Dr. Taylor's thesis that a pastor (a watchman) is in a much better position to speak God's Word to God's people if that pastor is a man or woman "of their own coasts."

As one who is cut from the same cloth of oppression, racism, and powerlessness which inner-city blacks experience, Trinity's pastor then works with the congregation to combine the words of Jesus: "Love thyself" and the dictum, "Know thyself," (erroneously ascribed to Socrates, but actually found on all ancient entry pillars guarding the temples of African mystery religions). These two teachings form the conceptual framework out of which Trinity operates as it attempts to build on the cultural strengths already present within the black community.

The unfortunate overarching motif of the black community is black self-hatred. It has been both overtly taught by and surreptitiously learned from the dominant culture for the past 100 years. It is characterized by the aspiration to European values in order to become Euro-Christian, or figuratively to be washed "whiter than snow." This motif negates our black cultural heritage and history and repeats (with the same amount of arrogance) the mistakes made by the first New England missionaries (Congregational,

Presbyterian, Episcopal, etc.) who tried to recreate African slaves in their own images.

Trinity rejects that model of ministry, and starts from the cultural strengths within the black tradition as it goes about its theological and evangelical tasks: modeling the ministry of Jesus, being faithful to the Great Commission, and respecting the economic level within the black community.

III. UNIQUELY URBAN

The factors that make Trinity's ministry uniquely urban are discernible both in its worship services and in its church programs. In the worship service, gospel music is the key urban phenomenon. Chicago is still the home and birthplace of gospel music, and at Trinity this reality is affirmed. The big choir sound of the 200-voice sanctuary choir, a crucial component of Trinity's worship services, is not something that could be easily duplicated in rural communities where entire congregations are hardly as large.

In addition to the worship services, church programs that address the powerlessness of blacks living in a sprawling, racist metropolitan setting also make Trinity's ministry uniquely urban. In a city where fresh fruits and produce do not even reach black community supermarkets for two weeks, Trinity, in cooperation with six other churches, is developing a food co-op which will provide these necessities one day after they arrive in the city, at a considerable savings in cost. In a city where inflation and the cost of living make money tight and where loans are almost out of reach for most blacks, Trinity has a credit union where the interest rate remains at 12 percent.

Two additional examples of this uniquely urban ministry are the housing ministry and the child-care program. The housing ministry is one of several board programs for long-range planning. It addresses the problem of abandoned and boarded-up houses lost by black homeowners through racist sales or financing policies, or through the inability of single-parent families to keep up the payments, taxes, and repairs required for residential properties. The housing ministry also combats the practice of redlining and continues to seek solutions for displaced families caught in the squeeze between urban renewal and regentrification (i.e. black removal).

The child-care program consists of two federally funded Title XX programs, Day Care and Head Start, running twelve months a year and ten months a year respectively. Both programs provide quality child care (from 7 a.m. until 6 p.m.) and educational fundamentals for black children ages two to five years whose parent or parents are below the poverty level and who are either unemployed (and in training) or underemployed. For many parents the cost of these services is little or nothing, depending on where they fall on the sliding scale set by the government.

In a city with a crippled and racist board of education, a school system that does not educate, and a pattern of school segregation that has produced the lowest reading scores in the nation among black school children, Trinity has a reading tutorial program guaranteed to raise a child's reading score one decimal point for every month that the child is enrolled in the program.

The Christian education program is also tailored to the needs of inner-city blacks. There are, for example, few rural communities that have to equip the saints for warfare against the heresies of the Universal Awareness movement (whose thousands of followers reject the theology of the cross and the divinity of Jesus and worship Rev. Ike, money, and hedonism), the Jehovah's Witnesses, and the Black Hebrews. Metropolitan living puts the congregation in daily contact with large numbers of these people in addition to other regular sects and cults. Trinity feels that its Christian education emphasis must take these conditions into account, or border on being totally irrelevant.

Political education is the final emphasis that makes Trinity's ministry more urban than rural. Liaisons between Chicago's political machine and Frazier's "Negro church" produced a number of illegitimate children—old-line "Negro leaders," patronage job holders, precinct captains, and others. Although one of their parents is dead, and the other parent is thrashing about violently on its deathbed, they still roam around as pretenders to a nonexistent throne. Educating constituents to all the nuances and subtleties of Chicago's racist political system and suggesting ways to address that system as free children of the most high king is a very definite part of the ministry at Trinity.

IV. STRUCTURE

The autonomous congregational polity of the United Church of Christ is the formal structure out of which Trinity operates. A constitution clearly outlines the duties and responsibilities of members, pastors, officers, boards, and councils. The constitution is reviewed periodically and revised when necessary to adapt the ministry of the church to the exigencies of a changing community, city, and world.

However, Trinity's informal structure and leadership style in many ways complement its formal structure, and all three combine forces to make the church what it has become.

The informal structure consists of the African-based extended family concept and the Nguzo Saba (or Seven Principles), which Trinity affirms as avowedly as the United Church of Christ's Statement of Faith. The following is a brief description of how these structures (formal and informal) complement each other.

Formally, the congregation has ultimate authority, or the final say. This compares with the African tribal structure where ultimate authority is vested in the collective wisdom of the tribe (see Chancellor Williams's *The Destruction of Black Civilization* for a full explanation of this concept).

According to Trinity's constitution, the pastor, once installed, is the administrative and spiritual head of the church. This is comparable to the African concept that tribal leadership is a sacred trust given to the chief by the tribe, who then holds the chief accountable for the careful exercise of that sacred trust. The congregation meets only quarterly so the management of church business, in consultation and conjunction with the pastor and his or her staff, is formally vested in the executive council and administrative committee which meet monthly. This structure parallels the Council of Elders, another African tribal concept.

Informally, the extended family structure empowers the congregational officials in two ways. First, the congregation is perceived and affirmed as a church *family*: there is a conscious effort to retain the love, warmth, and close-knit character of family life, no matter how large the congregation grows. Second, the concept of family precludes any notions of class, caste, or status. *Everybody* is somebody in this family, the Ph.Ds and those on A.D.C.

Positions of leadership (on boards, councils, committees, and as teachers) are shared equally by family members, whether or not they are recognized as leaders by the dominant culture.

The following are examples of this concept at work:

1) The pastor of the church has three earned degrees. His first assistant is still in the process of completing her first. Yet, they are respected as equals and as colleagues.

2) The chairperson of the executive council for the past seven years is a construction worker without a college degree; a past vice-chairperson is a trained structural engineer.

3) Recent co-chairpersons of the board of deacons were a supply clerk and a registered nurse with an M.S.

4) The director of Christian education has an M.R.E.; the past chairperson of the board of trustees is an electrician.

5) One adult Bible class teacher is a professional educator; another (her supervisor) is a service representative for Illinois Bell, and yet another is a homemaker. The broad spectrum of occupations within the educational unit reflects the diversity of the larger church body.

Degrees and so-called stations of life are matters of importance (for egos) *outside* the extended family; they pertain only to how one makes a living. One's relationship to Christ is what determines how one makes a life, and making a life in a community is one of the primary activities of an extended family. The representative form of government on official boards and on the executive council cuts across all socioeconomic and educational lines (just as church membership does) to ensure the continuity of a living family with mutual respect at every level of its formal hierarchy.

Trinity's congregation (and leadership) also shares a commitment to the communal goals of the Nguzo Saba (i.e., unity, self-determination, collective work and responsibility, cooperative economics, creativity, purpose, and faith), and the church works continuously to implement these goals. Because of the high trust levels implicit in the concepts both of the family and these seven principles, this informal structure solidifies the church as it goes about the work of the risen Christ in many new and exciting ways.

The leadership style at Trinity is dedicated to a trained laity, shared leadership responsibilities, and leadership development. More classes are offered to Trinity's members and officers than are sometimes found in several other churches put together. First, new members are given four hours of classes before they are received into the congregation. Second, more than twenty adult Bible classes are taught each week at the church ("The world is hungry for the living bread") in addition to the regular church school and

71

youth training programs.

Third, there are credit courses offered at university levels in areas such as black religion. These classes meet three hours per week for a ten-week period. Next, there are leadership development training workshops held throughout the year, every year, for the various elected officers. The board of deacons has ten hours of instruction annually in addition to training segments in its regular monthly meetings. The stewardship council has all-day workshops (9 a.m. to 5 p.m.) to train its members for their various roles and responsibilities. (Members of this council, incidentally, teach one of the three semi-monthly new member classes and are also trained to teach the other two.)

The executive council has an all-day (8 a.m. to 5 p.m.) leadership development workshop at the beginning of each year, a mid-year all-day retreat, and an hour and a half leadership development workshop five months of each year. Finally, in addition to various spiritual and educational retreats held for all segments of the church family each year (e.g., the men's fellowship retreat, music department retreats for adults and for grade children, and the singles, couples, women's fellowship, and board of deacon retreats), the board of Christian education requests that each organization spend ten to twenty minutes of its meetings in discussing some aspect of the annual all-church Christian education objective.

An educated clergy is only half the story: a trained laity and shared leadership responsibilities are what build self-perpetuating institutions in the name of Jesus.

V. PREPARATION

There are three prerequisites for ministry at Trinity: a knowledge of the black religious tradition; a familiarity with the black experience in the United States generally, and in Chicago specifically; and a genuine love for black people.

Knowing the black religious tradition inside and out is the first requirement for this model of black church renewal. Gayraud Wilmore's *Black Religion and Black Radicalism*, C. Eric Lincoln's *The Black Church Since Frazier*, James Cone's *God of the Oppressed*, and Wyatt Tee Walker's *Somebody's Calling My Name: Black Sacred Music and Social Change*, would all broaden one's understanding of the black tradition in religion.

In addition to this background, however, a pastor must also be able to structure a black worship service, sing in the black idiom (if possible), and most definitely preach in the black tradition. It is essential that these skills accompany any and all reading in the black church tradition. Having lived the black experience is helpful in terms of the second prerequisite (familiarity with the black experience), but its importance is secondary to these skills. There is a plethora of books on the black experience that could broaden one's perspectives in this direction. Talking and listening attentively to older blacks who have lived the black experience is also an invaluable supplement to reading.

The third prerequisite for developing this kind of ministry, a genuine love for black people, is perhaps the most important of all. By genuine, we mean a love for black people *as* black people, in all their possible variations. It is to feel just as comfortable with James Cleveland and Andraé Crouch as with Paul Tillich and Martin Noth, and to appreciate the Common Meter and Dr. Watts hymns *just* as much as (if not *more* than) Handel's *Messiah* or DuBois' "Seven Last Words."

One has to know, love, understand, appreciate, and accept the black lexicon and black English just as vividly as one tackled his or her Greek and Hebrew in seminary. *Only* a love for blacks *qua* blacks will prevent the clergy from attempting to make over in Anglo images the flock God gives them to serve. An understanding of the message of Jesus, divorced from the European cultural trappings which the African slaves heard and received is mandatory if this love is to be communicated to blacks *as they are*, culturally.

VI. EFFECTIVENESS

A recent evaluation at Trinity produced the following results:

1) In March of 1972, Trinity's congregation, then only ten years old and caught in the crosscurrents of sociological and psychological changes, had dwindled to eighty-seven dues-paying members. As of September 1982, there were more than 2,800 members.

2) Trinity's annual budget in 1972 was $39,000 (including $14,000 from members' out-of-pocket giving). As of 1982, the annual budget was $700,377, and out-of-pocket giving was more than $545,000.

3) From 1961 to 1971, the congregation (many of whom were chief mourners at the funeral of the "Negro church") produced only one candidate for the professional ministry. Between 1972 and 1982, Trinity ordained two pastors, licensed two more, and received into its church family three others through the UCC "Privilege of Call." As of September 1982, it had nine more students in seminary, and one recent graduate ready for ordination.

These three points are objective measures of Trinity's effectiveness. Another is found in the words of Dr. W. Sterling Cary, conference minister of the Illinois Conference of the United Church of Christ. In March, 1980, he reported that Trinity United Church of Christ in Chicago was the "fastest growing church in the entire denomination, which is composed of over 6,500 congregations."

Trinity United Church of Christ is only *one* of many, many models of black church renewal since 1960. Its work and story only begin to convey what the black church has done and is continuing to do, both in Chicago, and throughout the nation.

THE BACKGROUND OF THE U.S. IMMIGRATION POLICY TOWARD ASIANS
Implications for the Urban Church Today

Wi Jo Kang, professor, Wartburg Theological Seminary

One doesn't have to look too closely these days to see that the ethnic density of U.S. cities is rapidly changing. According to official government figures, between 1965 when the National Origins Act was passed and 1974 Asian immigration increased by 532 percent while European immigration declined by 73 percent.

For the most part, these Asian immigrants are finding their place in North American life. In many urban areas, hospitals are now largely staffed by Asian doctors and nurses. Each year a sizable number of small business licenses are granted to Asians. Asians are also among those who are renovating run-down urban areas to increase property values.

Still, the Asian-American experience has not been an unqualified success. Like many other minority peoples, Asians have often not been readily accepted by their new U.S. neighbors. Less affluent immigrants may find themselves isolated in Chinatowns. Asians who can afford to live in upper-middle-class suburbs may still have a difficult time mingling with their white neighbors. These associations tend to be superficial at best; at worst they are openly hostile.

The U.S. Christian community seems to reinforce many of these experiences. While Asia has traditionally been the focus of intense missionary activity, Asians are not generally welcomed into U.S. fellowships. Asians who graduate from seminary usually have a hard time finding places to serve in the United States or abroad.

On the corporate level, Asian-Christian churches often do not enjoy good administrative or ecclesiastical relationships with other U.S. churches. Asian-Christian churches tend to be small mission congregations that rent space from established churches. But many churches charge as much as fifty dollars for a simple church meeting, and they often refuse to provide office space for Asian pastors who minister to immigrants. One church on the Chicago's South Side does not allow the Asian pastor to use the pulpit when he preaches because the people of the church feel that it is improper.

It is our thesis that such attitudes can be seen, in part, as remnants of the United States government policy toward Asian immigrants. It is hoped that this data will lead to greater understanding between U.S. citizens and Asian immigrants, so that through mutual respect and appreciation, equal recognition, and Christian love, they may together build bright, reconciling, and joyous urban communities.

The United States government has traditionally encouraged immigration as a means of developing urban communities. This nation was literally built by immigrants. In its early years the United States had no formal immigration policy. According to the latest official pamphlet on "Development of Immigration and Naturalization Laws and Service History," distributed by the United States Department of Justice:

> For almost a hundred years after this nation was founded the federal laws did not incorporate any restriction against the admission of aliens. Our national policy then favored unrestricted immigration, and this policy was richly rewarded through the substantial contributions made by immigrants and their descendents in the building of this country.

In actual practice, this open welcome extended only to Europeans. With respect to East Asians, both state and federal governments adopted policies of overt discrimination.

Most early East Asian immigrants—the Chinese, Koreans, and Japanese—came to the U.S. as laborers. The earliest Chinese immigrants came to the U.S. soon after the gold rush of 1849 as a source of cheap labor for the mines. Before 1848, virtually no Chinese or other East Asians lived in the United States; after the gold rush their numbers soared.

This influx was due, in part, to trying conditions abroad. Nineteenth-century China was ravaged by disorder, war, rebellion, and unemployment. Many Chinese saw emigration as their only hope for a better life. Some Chinese emigrants were recruited by commercial agents, in a sort of employment and immigration brokerage. Agents often forced unwitting Chinese to sign contracts they couldn't read that bound them to labor for years at a time. The contracts were then sold to employers in the United States (Jacobs, 1971:77).

Many other Chinese came to the United States through the credit-ticket system arranged by labor recruiting agencies. These agencies advanced passage money to Chinese laborers who wanted to emigrate to the United States. Laborers were expected to repay the debt out of earnings made in their new home. Many agents made their fortunes in this way.

Life did not necessarily improve when the Chinese arrived in the United States. Wages were low in comparison to European immigrant pay scales, and economic burdens were compounded by civil restrictions and by selectively imposed tax laws. In 1855 an immigration tax was introduced on alien entry into California. This law was primarily imposed to discourage further Chinese immigration. Three years later, California imposed the Foreign Miner's Tax of 1858. This too was primarily directed against the Chinese to restrict economic activities in the gold mines. Chinese miners who refused to pay were beaten, stabbed, or shot. Sometimes Chinese laborers were tied to trees and whipped, or driven on foot with horsewhips. Under these conditions, Chinese immigration dropped from 16,000 in 1854, to 3,300 in 1855. For the next decade Chinese immigration continued to decline until the Chinese-American population stabilized at around 50,000, with the majority living in California (Jacobs, 1971:80).

By the 1860s, however, the need for Chinese laborers had once again increased. This time they were needed to build the transcontinental railroads. A Chinese labor force of 10,000 to 12,000 worked until 1869 to complete the railroad. One year after the project was finished, the federal government enacted the Naturalization Act of 1870, which restricted Chinese immigration and excluded naturalization of resident Chinese. Twelve years later, in 1882, the government adopted the first Chinese Exclusion Act which prohibited Chinese wives from joining their husbands in the United States. Most Chinese laborers left home expecting that their families would eventually be reunited. The effects of this law were particularly devastating. In connection with the prohibition against bringing wives of the Chinese laborers, the Anti-Miscegenation Action Law of California was passed in 1906, which prohibited marriages between Caucasians and Chinese (Park, 1975:27). In 1892, the federal government passed the Geary Act which enjoined all Chinese immigration and naturalization from 1892 to 1902. In 1902, Congress extended the Geary Act indefinitely. This act remained in effect until 1943 when President Franklin D. Roosevelt repealed it because of the alliance between the United States and China in the Second World War.

Government immigration policy towards the Chinese both reflected and reinforced public opinion. There was widespread feeling that the Chinese were cruel people without reverence for life. It was generally believed that they were dirty, unsanitary, diseased, and germ-ridden. In 1854, Horace Greeley of the *New York Tribune* wrote:

> The Chinese are uncivilized, unclean and filthy beyond all conception without any of the higher domestic or social relations; lustful and sensual in their dispositions; every female is a prostitute of the basest order (quoted in Jacobs, 1971:93).

This hostility often erupted into open violence. In the 1880s there were widespread anti-Chinese riots in many cities of the United States. In Rock Springs, Wyoming, white miners killed twenty-eight Chinese and burned hundreds of others out of their homes. Public attitudes found their way into official state and federal documents. The following was part of a report made by California's State Board of Health in 1871:

> Better it would be for our country that the hordes of Genghis Khan should overflow the land, and with armed hostility devastate our valley with the sabre and firebrand than that these more pernicious hosts in the garb of friends, should insidiously poison the wellsprings of life, and spreading far and wide, gradually undermine and corrode the vitals of our strength and prosperity. In the former instance, we might oppose the invasion with sword and rifled cannon, but this destructive intrusion enters by invisible approaches. . . (Jacobs, 1971:99).

A similar theme appears in the 1882 Chinese Exclusion Act:

> Whereas, in the opinion of the Government of the United States the coming of Chinese laborers to this country endangers the good order of certain localities within the territory thereof. . . . That hereafter no State court or court of the United States shall admit Chinese to citizenship. . . (Jacobs, 1971:100).

United States immigration policy toward other East Asians was essentially similar to the Chinese, especially for the Japanese. As one Stanford University scholar pointed out: "The Japanese inherited the prejudice against the Chinese" (Ichihashi, 1969:228). Like the Chinese, the Japanese came to the United States as cheap labor, but they were relative latecomers in comparison to the Chinese and their numbers were small. Still, their coming did not escape public attention. A California politician writing in 1886 complained that:

> Wherever the Japanese have settled, their nests pollute the communities like the running sores of leprosy. They exist like the yellow, smoldering discarded butts in an over-full ashtray, vilifying the air with their loathsome smells, filling all those who have the misfortune to look upon them with a wholesome disgust and a desire to wash (Jacobs, 1971:170).

In 1901, the State of California adopted a joint resolution and forwarded a memorandum to Congress asking for the restriction of Japanese immigration. In support of this legislation, California governor, Henry G. Gagy, advised the state legislature that:

> The peril from Chinese labor finds a similar danger in the unrestricted immigration of Japanese laborers. The cheapness of that labor is likewise a menace to American labor, and a new treaty with Japan for such restriction, as well as the passage of laws by Congress, is desired for the protection of Americans. I therefore most earnestly appeal to your honorable bodies for the passage as a matter of urgency of appropriated resolutions instructing our Senators and requesting our representatives in Congress for the immediate institution of all proper measures leading to the revision of the existing treaties with China and Japan, and the passage of all necessary laws and resolutions for the protection of American labor against the immigration of oriental laborers (Ichihashi, 1969:231).

Many of the forces opposed to Japanese immigration joined together in 1905 to organize the Asiatic Exclusion League. The League's basic objective was expressed as "the preservation of the Caucasian race upon American soil and particularly upon the Western soil thereof, [which] necessitates the adoption of all measures to prevent or minimize the immigration of Asiatics to America" (Jacobs, 1971:174). Largely as a result of their efforts, in 1907 Congress granted the president authority to limit admission to only those Japanese who had passports originally drawn for entry into the United States.

By the end of the First World War, increased immigration pressures made it impossible to maintain an unrestricted immigration policy even toward Europeans. As a result, the government enacted a new immigration law, the Quota Act of 1921. According to the Quota Act, the number of persons admitted annually from any one country was not to exceed 3 percent of that nationality resident in the United States in 1910, based on official census figures for that year. In 1924, Congress adopted another significant immigration statute, the Permanent Quota Act. This law regulated the admission and deportation of aliens and limited quota immigrants to about 150,000 each year. It also changed the baseline year for such quotas from 1910 to 1920.

This new quota act did not materially affect European immigration. It is often jokingly said that the Irish never had enough immigrants to meet the quota limit. But since earlier legislation worked to exclude East Asians, the number of East Asians living in the United States in 1920 was disproportionately low. The Quota Act only aggravated this situation. The implication of this system was correctly pointed out by Dr. William S. Bernard, the executive director of the American Federation of International Institutes in New York:

> . . . The concept of National Origins determines the size of the quotas allocated to the various countries of the world. And since the countries of northern and western Europe receive some 82 percent of the total quota, it is obvious that National Origins accords them superior status. Conversely, southern and eastern Europeans, Asiatics, Africans, inhabitants of Oceania. . . are inferior, receiving the scanty and token quota remaining (Bernard, 1959:66-67).

Conditions improved somewhat in 1950, with the passage of the McCarren-Walter Act. This law allowed Asians to become naturalized United States citizens (Park, 1975:27), but did nothing to alter the Quota Act of 1924.

In 1965, the Quota Act was finally abolished in favor of the National Origins Act. According to this new law, all nationalities from all parts of the world may immigrate and be naturalized on an equal basis (Park: 1975:27). This new law was signed by President Johnson with great ceremony at the Statue of Liberty in New York Harbor. (Some suggest that he should have signed it in San Francisco.)

While Asian immigrants are no longer targets of restrictive government policies, they still encounter social barriers. The new challenge is for Asians and North Americans to work together to build pluralistic communities of harmony and peace. The Christian church could be paramount in this task.

Indeed, there is historical precedent for this kind of interaction. Some U.S. pastors and lay leaders did initiate church programs for Asians in the early years of Chinese and Japanese immigration. By 1859, R.W.A. Speer, a former medical missionary to China, had opened a medical clinic for his San Francisco congregation. The following year a Baptist preacher, the Rev. J.S. Shuck, formed a Chinese church in Sacramento. A Chinese Methodist church was founded in San Francisco in 1868, by the Rev. Otis Gibson; and in 1873, a Chinese Congregational church was started by the Rev. William C. Pond in San Francisco. Among Japanese immigrants Dr. E.A. Sturge established a Presbyterian congregation in the same city. In 1906, a Korean church was started in Los Angeles by the Koreans themselves.

Most of these examples, however, were exceptions to the rule. Historically, while some few church leaders were attentive to Asian needs for the Gospel and for community services, most mainstream Christian churches supported restrictive government policies and shared the anti-Asian sentiment behind them. Asians who worked in U.S. denominations had little voice in the decision-making process even about the church's work among Asian-American immigrants and denominational missions in immigrant homelands. It was often difficult for Asian pastors and church workers to find jobs in mainline denominations. When they did, their salaries did not match those of their white colleagues. It is still hard for qualified Asian pastors and scholars to locate work in U.S. churches and denominations. It is this frustration that leads many Asian church leaders to form ethnic congregations apart from the white Christian community. This ecclesiastical segregation further insulates Asians from the day-to-day contact with other North Americans that could help them learn about and adjust to their new life.

Thus, some practical suggestions for urban ministry among Asian immigrants, both Christian and non-Christian, might include looking for ways to initiate friendships, setting up English classes, helping recent arrivals orient themselves in new neighborhoods, and inviting them to Christian worship. Many non-Christian Asian immigrants are not accustomed to the idea of weekly worship services. In the Orient, temples are always open for individual or family worship. Some Asians may expect the same of churches and request entry for worship and prayer in the middle of the night or the early morning. These situations are natural opportunities to share our Christian faith. A final suggestion, and perhaps the most important, is that U.S. pastors and lay Christians take time to learn about their Asian-American neighbors. There is much that could be more widely understood and appreciated about the special needs and concerns of Asian-Americans, Asian cultural and religious heritage, and Asian contributions to U.S. life. Organizations such as the Seminary Consortium for Urban Pastoral Education (SCUPE) might initiate Asian ministry studies that could lead to such educational programs.

Asian-Americans fully and joyously integrated into U.S. life would be an undeniable witness to the cities of the reality of the kingdom.

REFERENCES CITED

Bernard, William S. 1959. American Immigration Policy in the Era of the Dispossessed. *Social Work*. January.

Gordon, Charles. 1972. *Development of Immigration and Naturalization Laws and Service History*. Washington: U.S. Department of Justice.

Ichihashi, Yamato. 1969. *Japanese in the United States*. New York: Arno Press.

Jacobs, Paul, et. al. 1971. *To Serve the Devil*. New York: Vantage Books.

Park, Philip K.S. 1975. Asian Christians and the Bicentennial. *Bicentennial Broadside*. New York: National Council of Churches.

STRATEGIES OF MINISTRY AND EVANGELIZATION FOR THE URBAN CHURCH

MINISTRY ON THE URBAN FRONTIER: ACCESS AND RETIREMENT

Philip Amerson, director, Patchwork Central Ministries

PROLOGUE

The Dynamic of the Urban Frontier

Most North Americans would probably agree that the frontier is a thing of the past. Certainly, if one thinks in terms of open land and westward settlement, those days are gone, but perhaps we are overlooking contemporary frontiers. It may well be that preconceived notions about westward expansion and virgin territory mask some of the emerging frontiers of our society. Because of this confusion, North Americans seem determined to repeat many of the same development patterns that scarred the first frontier. Our postindustrial society is one of increasingly complex options. New technologies, multinational commerce and capital development, and shifting military styles and alignments all suggest that we have entered a new era of growth whose course now depends on technology and imagination, rather than on territorial expansion.

It is in our cities that these new signposts are most clearly visible. Here, growth and change have created their own vocabularies, with terms like gentrification, disinvestment, revitalization and displacement. In the last two decades of the twentieth century, the city will in fact be the reigning frontier, with new populations, new work trends, and new lifestyles. As grandchildren and great-grandchildren of our original European immigrants pour into core city neighborhoods, social processes in effect during the early settlement of the United States are being replayed on the urban frontier. One pattern, the displacement of indigenous populations, is occurring just as surely today as it did among native North Americans a century ago. Not only are these urban tribes being forced out of their city homelands, but traditional institutions are likewise giving way to the institutions of the newest immigrants. A middle class new to the cities is displacing at least two generations of low and moderate income families. Phenomena such as displacement, domination, and resettlement are increasingly common today.

This state of flux is but one of an increasing range of challenges and prospects that face the urban church as hundreds of neighborhoods across the

United States undergo transition. Local churches must make difficult decisions about how, and indeed if, they can maintain ongoing ministries to the poor and to minorities and still meet the needs of the new urban gentry.

The mainline church has never really established itself among the city's poor and minority populations. Moreover, since most of the new urban middle class neither attend church nor profess individual faith, it is unlikely that the mainline church will find much success here either. It may well be that as the process of secularization continues in our society, the role of the traditional church with both groups will become increasingly marginal. Thus the crucial issue of ministry today is how to develop new avenues of access to populations that seem to lie outside the reach of the traditional church.

It might be helpful at this point to consider some of the methods by which other church groups and religious movements have gained access for ministry. One example that comes to mind is the great Wesleyan revival of nineteenth-century frontier North America. This powerful movement suggests a number of possible elements of theology, scale, style, and group size that might also be appropriate for the contemporary frontier. Another possible model comes from the Latin American groups known as *Las Comunidades Eclesiales de la Base*—"Church Communities of the Base" (Sand, 1980:14-19; International Review of Missions, 1979; Cook, 1980:20-23). It is estimated that from 150,000 to 160,000 of these small groups now exist throughout Latin America. Interestingly enough, they are in many respects quite similar to the house churches of eighteenth- and nineteenth-century Methodism—small, adaptable to the concerns of a particular neighborhood and people, and guided by indigenous leaders who are supported by an itinerant ministry.

As John Vincent argues:

> We need to learn how to set up small churches from the bottom. The beginnings of Methodism were in small groups of people whom Wesley gathered together in a particular place, for whom he appointed a leader, and which he serviced by an itinerant semi-full-time or part-time ministry. The genius of Methodism was that at a particular time in history we were able to create appropriate mini-forms of the Christian church, and to insist that all the charismata and the means of grace should be available to people from those among whom they lived, in each other's houses, sustaining fellowship, discipline, economics and sacramental life in small nuclear groups. Anyone who reads John Wesley's *Journal* will know how greatly he hesitated about the erection of buildings which would take larger groups of people. . . it was the tragedy of Methodism toward the end of John Wesley's life and throughout the 19th century that the notion was taken over of the church as a building within a particular area, serviced by a professional ministry, and depending upon the financial support of fairly large groups of people (Vincent, 1977:4-5).

It now seems clear that a new urban climate is emerging and the value of understanding its unique demographical and cultural character is all too obvious. However, it is even more important that the church begin to initiate imaginative and dynamic new models of ministry for the urban frontier. The urban frontier is in fact a study in perpetual motion, acutely sensitive to political, economic, social, and cultural pressures. Rather than being a stronghold of the status quo or a base from which the church conducts business as usual, the urban frontier demands churches that are centers of creativity, starting points of exploration, and outposts of initiative.

If these thoughts can be said to fall under a theological rubric, they are perhaps most closely related to a North American variety of liberation theology. For one thing, the dynamic of an urban frontier clearly requires theological reflection within a specific context. For another, the practice of urban ministry will most often precede the actual drafting of theological premises, so that experience itself becomes the grist for proposition. Effective ministry outreach to the urban frontier will depend on planning that begins with human reality and not with a planner's text. It will encourage neighborhood-based land use rather than open-market development. It will seek to redirect gentrification so that the urban poor are not consigned to patrolled reservations in the suburbs; and it will develop reinvestment alternatives that expand the economic choices of persons now living in urban neighborhoods. Finally, it will insist on theologies rooted in the everyday experiences of urban life.

The Dialectic of Access and Retirement

One helpful way of discussing ministry and theology on the urban frontier is to speak in terms of a dialectic of access and retirement. By access we mean the ability of the church to be in contact with the many different kinds of people who populate contemporary urban neighborhoods. By retirement we mean the sensitivity that allows ministry and ministers to know the appropriate time of their own leave-taking. A brief discussion of these two concepts might be useful at this point.

Access refers specifically to the way the church relates to those people who traditionally have had little or no contact with the church or its ministries (Amerson, 1979). It is probably safe to assume that any ministry with an adequate theology of the incarnation will understand the importance of bringing together people of diverse groups and perspectives. Certainly, the metaphor of the body of Christ suggests that a multiplicity of persons and talents should make up the church.

One of the fascinating ironies of postindustrial North America is that while communication and transportation are two of our most rapidly advancing technologies, they act more to separate people who are different than to connect people who differ. For example, the automotive industry reinforces our desire for individual mobility and we shun mass transportation even though it is unquestionably more efficient. We are, in many respects, a much more segregated society today than we were just twenty years ago. And this segregation is not only racial or ethnic. Our cities are increasingly composed of separate homogeneous clusters. We find areas almost completely given over to elderly persons, or to persons of a specific income bracket or lifestyle, or to persons who are single or married, or to those with children. It is important—theologically important—that the church gives all these people natural and frequent access to one another. This unifying function is upheld by Paul in his letters to the urban dwellers of his day (see

Galatians 3 and Ephesians 2). Mainline middle-class churches in particular need these cross-cultural contacts if they are to integrate the symbol of the incarnation into the experience of everyday life.

Mainline churches, if they are truly to be the church, must also reconsider their responsibility to the urban poor. Jesus came as a poor man, living with poor people. The Gospel makes it very clear that God's word and purposes were directed first of all to the poor.

Christian access has little or no relationship to agent/client relationships, dominant/subordinate interactions, or bureaucratic power structures. Unfortunately, many of our theological schools promote these professional styles which more often than not reinforce depersonalization. Access involves making and keeping covenants in a spirit of mutuality and trust, not the assumption of competing interests and implicit threats.

The process of gaining access is not without its dangers. For many who approach urban ministry with powerful organizational backing, the process of gaining access all too often ends in dominance. This dominance, though unintended and unrecognized, is nonetheless real. Seeking access is risky unless the quest is accompanied by sensitivity about when and how to properly retire.

The notion of Christian retirement is affirmed in Roland Allen's, *Missionary Methods: St. Paul's or Ours?* Allen notes that Paul practiced retirement not by constraint but by willingly giving up positions of control over the lives of early Christians and their churches. Paul, according to Allen, welcomed the independence of those with whom he had shared the Gospel.

> He gave freely and then he retired from them that they might learn to exercise the powers which they possessed in Christ. He warned them of dangers, but he did not provide an elaborate machinery to prevent them from succumbing to the dangers (Allen, 1962).

Allen goes on to argue that we need to subordinate our methods, our systems, and ourselves to a faith that Christ is able and willing to keep what was committed to him. Retirement demonstrates our belief that what systems, forms, and safeguards of every kind cannot do, God can do. Christian retirement is neither abandonment nor passive retreat, but a voluntary step back to allow space for others. It is a statement of faith about the possibility of ongoing relationships both among people, and between people and God. Undertaken at a point where others are on the verge of new opportunities, retirement is synergistic and energizing. It is a sign not of self-effacement, but of mutual respect stemming from a common covenant.

A Biblical Model

The incarnation of Jesus is the ultimate expression of God's desire to be accessible to human beings. Access to our flesh and blood is made through the physical presence of Jesus Christ in the world. Yet it is also clear from the gospel accounts that there is a pattern of both retirement and access in Jesus' ministry. During the Galilean ministry, and later, on the journey to Jerusalem, Jesus moved almost in counterpoint between being accessible to people and then withdrawing or retiring from them.

Perhaps too much has been made of the idea that discipleship always means literally following Jesus (Schweizer, 1970; Schweizer, 1960: 11-21). Relatively few believers actually followed Jesus throughout his entire ministry; even those who did found themselves suddenly alone at the crucifixion.

There is considerable conjecture among New Testament commentaries about the reasons behind Jesus' voluntary absences. Most suggest that Jesus retired because he needed to pray, meditate, and renew his own spiritual powers. However, a neglected corollary of this assumption may be that Jesus also withdrew for the benefit of the crowd, in order to discourage dependency and false commitments based on his miraculous powers. Retirement was so completely integrated into Jesus' schedule that ministry was never just a matter of gaining access and being with people. Once access was achieved and the word or the act was accomplished, Jesus went his way. This behavior, in one who personified absolute access to humankind, continually surprised Jesus' followers. In his day-to-day ministry, in the crucifixion, and even in the resurrection the followers were caught off guard as Jesus moved beyond them. The resurrection is announced as *"Surrexit Dominus!"* "He is not here, he is risen!" (Mark 16:6; Matthew 28:6). A recurring theme of John's gospel is Jesus' hope-filled promise "I will go away but I will not leave you alone" (John 7:33-36; 8:21; 12:33-36; 16:7,10,28). Retirement complements access and for his followers, even Jesus' retirement is grace-*full*.

Christians who undertake urban ministries are often far more concerned about gaining access to people than they are about leaving when the right time comes. Nevertheless, access by itself is not sufficient for discipleship. If discipleship is to progress, those who have come in the power of the Word must retire so that faith can be directed to Christ and not to the message-bearer. Retirement may be as crucial for Christian growth as access, because without retirement faith may be diverted to ministers with special skills, plans, or abilities. Access with retirement helps new believers to place their faith where it truly belongs—in the power of the Holy Spirit.

PARABLES IN MIRACLES: THE DEMONIAC

> Then they arrived at the country of the Gerasenes, which is opposite Galilee. And as he stepped out on land, there met him a man from the city who had demons; for a long time he had worn no clothes, and he lived not in a house but among the tombs. When he saw Jesus, he cried out and fell down before him, and said with a loud voice, "What have you to do with me, Jesus, Son of the Most High God? I beseech you, do not torment me." For he had commanded the unclean spirit to come out of the man. (For many a time it had seized him; he was kept under guard, and bound with chains and fetters, but he broke the bonds and was driven by the demon into the desert.) Jesus then asked him, "What is your name?" And he said, "Legion"; for many demons had entered him. And they begged him not to command them to depart into the abyss. Now a large herd of swine was feeding there on the hillside; and they begged him to let them enter these. So he gave them leave. Then the demons came out of the man and entered the swine, and the herd rushed down the steep bank into the lake and were drowned.

> When the herdsmen saw what had happened, they fled, and told it in the city and in the country. Then people went out to see what had happened, and they came to Jesus, and found the man from whom the demons had gone, sitting at the feet of Jesus, clothed and in his right mind; and they were afraid. And those who had seen it told them how he who had been possessed with demons was healed. Then all the people of the surrounding country of the Gerasenes asked him to depart from them; for they were seized with great fear; so he got into the boat and returned. The man from whom the demons had gone begged that he might be with him; but he sent him away, saying, "Return to your home and declare how much God has done for you." And he went away, proclaiming throughout the whole city how much Jesus had done for him (Luke 8:26-39).

The gospel story of the Gerasene Demoniac is most instructive in terms of the motif of access and retirement. Recorded in all of the synoptic gospels, the story is told a bit differently in each. In Matthew it is said that Jesus met two men who were demon possessed; Mark's shorter version contains details not found in Matthew or Luke. Plutarcho Bonilla, in *Los milagros tambien son parabolas*, takes a look at the allegorical power of miracle stories in the New Testament. Although Bonilla's original intent was to investigate a number of miracle stories, the book, in fact, presents only two: the story of the great confession of Peter, and the story of the demon-possessed man (Bonilla, 1978). The story of the Gerasene Demoniac occupies most of the volume and one can only agree with the author that this material offers significant insight for the development of modern urban ministry.

In looking at the story of the Demoniac, one is struck by the parallels with modern urban life. Persons familiar with the enormous destructive character of poor urban neighborhoods can't help but sense here the comparable plight of the demon-possessed man. He is said to have had no clothing, no housing, to have been living in a place of death, and to have been kept chained under guard. The enormous power and vitality of the demon-possessed one is frequently turned to his own self-destruction.

It is also clear from this story that change comes only at a cost. The price of a hopeful future for one who once lived in the tombs was a herd of swine. Those who understand the dynamics of urban neighborhoods know that changing, moving, and assisting neighborhoods through transition also occurs at some expense. This passage also shows how hard it was for those nearby to accept the healing of the Demoniac. Apparently they had seen him attempt to leave the tombs many times before without success. Now, they not only feared him but they also projected their own evil onto this trapped one. Better to leave him chained among the dead than to risk having him free, better to watch him tear himself to pieces than to pay the costs of his return.

What is so unique about this story is that after the healing occurs, and after the Demoniac is released from the powers of destruction, his request to accompany Jesus is denied! Looking at the Demoniac, Jesus says, "No, don't come with me, go home to your friends in the city and tell them how much the Lord has done for you."

This New Testament story illustrates most dramatically the interplay between access and retirement. Jesus demonstrates not only the absolute necessity of gaining access for healing and ministry, but also the crucial need to move on to give people the responsibility to speak for themselves and to speak the gospel word for themselves.

This story stands in rather stark contrast to some understandings of discipleship that would have us walk in the footsteps of Jesus. According to this account, following Jesus for the Demoniac meant not proceeding with Jesus on the same path, but taking the message of Jesus down another road to his own neighborhood.

Expanding Our Definition: Parabolic Lessons

There are several lessons from this miracle story that bear directly on our understanding of the ministries of access and retirement.

1) Access means making contact with those who are outside the normal flow of ecclesiastical traffic. Jesus stopped by the tombs of the city.

2) Gaining access means asking for a name. Those who work in urban communities understand the importance of this concept. Names of persons, of clubs, and of communities all carry potential humanity. Identifying a person or group by name is a powerful way of moving toward access. Paulo Friere, in *Pedagogy of the Oppressed*, identifies the crucial function of allowing persons to name their own worlds (Friere, 1974). "Consciencization" allows people to express their own self-discoveries by naming them.

3) Gaining access means learning the complexity of human needs and understanding that there may be no simple solutions. The name which is provided is Legion; it is complexity. There are many names, the problems are multifaceted. Access suggests working to unify persons or communities which have been divided. Healing, too, requires diverse therapies. Neither funding, nor government aid, nor individual spiritual renewal, nor employment programs are sufficient by themselves. Only a whole range of ministries will allow the church to christen our city neighborhoods and peoples, giving them new and Christian names.

4) Gaining access means casting out demons, that is, taking aggressive intervention against the forces of evil in personal or community life.

5) People who saw Jesus' miracles were oftentimes so threatened that they asked him to leave before problems could be resolved.

6) Retirement means telling those who are healed to go back to the city and to take responsibility for themselves.

7) Retirement means giving people power over their own lives and then moving out of the way so they have the freedom to exercise that power. This power will not be based on existing political systems, for "Bureaucracy lives on control, but communities become self energizing only through escape from it" (Doughton, 1980:22).

TODAY'S DRAMA: TECHNIQUES APPLIED, MIRACLES DENIED

Jacques Ellul has persuasively argued that technology is the new substitute for faith (Ellul, 1964). Christian access and retirement are the children of faith and intuition, not of technical analysis. In a small treatise entitled *de Idolatria,* Tertullian asserted that there was in his time hardly any business or profession in which a Christian would not encounter idolatry in one form or another. Even today there appear to be few jobs in which Christians will not be tempted to substitute the idols of technology and bureaucratic control for the response of faith. The irony of the modern world, as stated earlier, is that technology serves more often to obstruct access than to enhance it, especially among persons who differ. When the church favors existing ministry techniques, miracles of access and retirement are often denied.

We have only to look at the contemporary urban scene to see some of the ways in which miracles of access are being undermined. For example, it has been suggested that until Christians actually join the poor in city neighborhoods, we will see few significant urban ministries. Sometimes it is simply not enough for one's heart to be in the right place. For the Christian it might be necessary for one's body to be in the right place as well. Living with the poor and interacting day by day with different kinds of people is no guarantee of effective ministry, but it does provide options for ministry that those who live outside the city simply do not have. Mutual sharing of such problems as inadequate transportation, police services, public schools, and recreation programs brings awareness of the names of the urban demons. It is not a sharing of the impotent but a communion of people who care, joining their resources to redirect the power which brings healing to our neighborhoods.

One need not look too closely at the involvements of most mainline denominations to understand that ecclesiastical redlining and outlining are common occurrences. The modern church too often prefers the techniques of church planting in urban communities rather than seeking the miracles of access. Modern research techniques have led many denominational leaders to conclude that churches are most likely to succeed where congregations are homogeneous units and middle-class worship patterns and world views can be maintained.

It is disturbing to realize that annual conferences in the United Methodist Church plan new ministries with the understanding that each new congregation comes with a price tag of $300,000. This kind of thinking (shared by many other denominations) is not only heavily biased by middle-class definitions of the church, but it is also remarkably out of step with the ministry spirit of nineteenth-century Methodism. This ecclesiastical redlining means that dollars needed to begin new ministries in core city neighborhoods are diverted to other supposedly more promising areas. Accepted church growth wisdom dictates that new ministries will not work in the inner city, and that the church is best understood as a middle-class institution with the large buildings, the full-time paid staff, and the programming we have come to expect in suburban churches.

In urban areas, gaining access will mean church workers who live and work in core city neighborhoods, and church resources that are directed to specific neighborhood needs. Access means that the church will provide natural and frequent opportunities for intimate interaction among community members. Increasing numbers of storefront and house churches in core city neighborhoods indicate that there are viable alternatives to the suburban church model. Nevertheless, mainline denominations tend to ignore this kind of growth because it represents a pattern of church life that does not fit into existing denominational categories.

Access cannot be gained by bringing in an external agenda and expecting people to adopt that agenda. Access cannot be made if those who seek to minister come with preconceived understandings of the names of people of our cities. If the demons are to be cast out, we must allow persons in our core city neighborhoods to name themselves and to name their world.

Urban ministry contains stumbling blocks to retirement as well as to access. The temptation is always present for community leaders to become spokespersons for the people rather than letting the people speak for themselves. In a recent meeting with city officials one young community organizer was heard to suggest that agreements made in the meeting need not become public too quickly. Having assumed power and control he now spoke as a superordinate on behalf of inferiors. How quickly leaders forget the responsibility to be with the people and not to answer for them. When organizers do not understand the appropriate time to retire, they deny neighborhood residents the power, the opportunity, and the freedom to speak for themselves.

Those who work in urban ministry need to learn to set aside any special techniques and technologies that separate them from the people they serve. Effective communication of the Gospel depends on discarding old patterns of dominance and subordinance. If we are truly interested in gaining access, urban ministry can no longer afford to operate out of past assumptions, styles, or structures. It is time to think of urban people less as clients and more as neighbors with names, histories, and futures apart from our own agendas.

Perhaps nothing so clearly illustrates the encroachment of past structures on present realities as the large old church buildings that dot our core city landscapes. These outdated, expensive museums are the temples of the if-onlys. Typically, the remaining few members of these urban fortresses spend their waning days crying, "If only we had moved," or "If only we had a better preacher," or "If only those neighborhood people would come in here." One must remember that it was not the neighborhood people who built the walls. It is not the neighborhood people who continue to close and lock the doors. It is not the neighborhood people who designate the programs of that church. If the church is to have ministry with frontier people, it must go beyond its walls, open its doors, and redesign its programming. In short, it must become an outpost.

The drama of urban ministry will continue to be played out both in the core city and in the suburbs. In each of these locations the question is increasingly becoming one of how congregations can be in touch with and readily available to the needy in their own midst. With today's increasing population shifts it is not at all unlikely that both core city and suburban churches, if they truly reflect their neighborhood compositions, will come to include all classes and all races. If the church is to remain viable in the city, it will be necessary that the cast, the plot, and the scriptwriters all seek appropriate styles of access and retirement.

TOMORROW'S HOPE: PARABLES ENFLESHED

The healing of the Demoniac offers several points of hope to the church that searches out new channels of ministry. Even in the presence of death among the tombs, there is hope for the church that listens as its people name themselves and their universe. As the church discovers the complexity of the urban world and comes to understand the patterns of interaction, the resources, and the problems of urban living, it can begin to model new ministries of healing and unity. The role of the church will be to intervene aggressively, to cast out the demons of the urban world, and to seek the unification and repersonalization of the city.

The Gospel of Mark mentions that Jesus returned to the cities of Decapolis (7:31-37) some time after the healing of the Demoniac. In contrast to his earlier reception, this time the people of the region were pleased to see Jesus and were eager to hear him and see his miracles among them. What changed their minds about Jesus? Perhaps it is not too far-fetched to suggest that the healed Demoniac Jesus left behind had by his own ministry introduced the people of his city to Jesus (Bonilla, 1978:140).

Contemporary disciples are also proclaiming Jesus on their urban frontier and here too there are hopeful signs of change. First there is the development of new models for old churches. There are numerous options for the large old churches that still abound in core city neighborhoods. Some buildings might need to be sold or torn down or given over to other uses, but others suggest the possibility of developing larger parishes both within denominations and across denominational lines. Opening old buildings for community use encourages the neighborhood to see the church as a resource rather than as a recluse. Older congregations must be willing to retire when the time comes, though for some the time appears to be long past. In this voluntary death, we have the opportunity to practice the resurrection as well as preach it.

A second sign of hope is the emergence of small nontraditional church groups. From house churches to storefront churches to Bible study groups, cities are full of cell groups similar to the grass-roots communities of Latin America. In these groups the parable of access and retirement is lived out day by day. Small in scale, personal in nature, and responsive to individual and community needs, these core groups are another clear signal of hope.

A third encouragement is found in the common involvement of Christians both from small groups and large old churches, in the struggle for healthy community renewal. In this struggle, as in individual interaction, gaining access is a key objective. It is primarily as churches gain political influence in school boards, county commissions, social welfare agencies, public health centers, and city councils that they are able to shape the future of urban neighborhoods. Churches may redirect urban growth in two ways: first by proposing renewal plans that preserve neighborhood character and discourage high cost and high technology developments; and second, by enlisting maximum community participation in planning and executing development projects more in scale with local needs and interests. (This is, after all, one way communities name themselves.) It is important that churches lend support to neighborhood-based economic and housing developments so that impetus for renewal comes from community action rather than by bureaucratic edict. Finally, the church needs to gain expertise in the key issues of modern urban life: gentrification and displacement, redlining and reinvestment, housing rehabilitation, condominium development, mixed-income housing patterns, and inadequate public education.

As they pursue these activities, Christians will need the support and critique of other believers similarly committed to community ministries of access and retirement. Retirement, in this larger social context, acts to curb the heresy that human efforts to reform human institutions will eradicate evil in the world. Retirement also helps to ensure that those who do attain positions of influence do not also lose touch with neighborhood constituents. Retirement means stepping outside the corridors of power to renew contact with the poor and oppressed. It also means retiring to communities of faith to pray and meditate before moving on.

Relinquishing power may in fact be the only road of access to the powerless. One friend recently decided to give only two hours a week to sitting on city panels and advisory boards in part because he was in danger of becoming the city's token representative of the poor. All too often, it is the advocates of the poor who are the very ones to lose contact with them.

And so the miracle of Jesus' restoration of the Demoniac becomes a parable of ministry in the city. Like the Demoniac, the urban poor of today have inadequate clothing and poor housing. They live in the presence of death, and are denied basic rights and freedoms. They turn their power inward to destroy themselves, and their healing is costly to the rest of the community. They are rejected and misunderstood, and are defenseless against the evils projected on them by society.

And we may ask, "Lord, can we follow you?" thinking to find the path cleared, marked, and tended by the traditional church, only to have Jesus reply, "If you want to follow me, then go and tell the people of your city what I have done. Understand that I will go away, but my Holy Spirit will continue with you. Restore my people, and I will return to your city and rejoice."

REFERENCES CITED

Allen, Roland. 1962. *Missionary Methods: St. Paul's or Ours?* Grand Rapids: Eerdmans.

Amerson, Philip. 1979. Excess or Access. *Sojourners.* July.

Bonilla, Plutarco. 1978. *Los milagros tambien son parabolas.* Miami: Editorial Caribe.

Cook, William. 1980. From a Hand-Carved Dove, a Call to Repentance. *The Other Side.* April: 20-23.

Doughton, Morgan J. 1980. People Power: An Alternative to Runaway Bureaucracy. *The Futurist.* April.

Ellul, Jacques. 1964. *The Technological Society.* New York: Knopf.

Friere, Paulo. 1974. *Pedagogy of the Oppressed.* New York: Seabury.

International Review of Missions. 1979. *Mission Without Missions?* Geneva: World Council of Churches.

Sand, Faith Annette, and William Cook. Winds of Change in Latin America. *The Other Side.* April.

Schweizer, Eduard. 1960. Following Jesus. *Lordship and Discipleship. Studies in Biblical Theology,* no. 28. London: SCM.

———. 1970. *The Good News According to Mark.* Atlanta: John Knox.

Vincent, John J. 1977. *Strategies for Misson.* Sheffield, England: Urban Theological Unit.

BARRIERS AND BRIDGES TO EVANGELIZATION IN URBAN NEIGHBORHOODS

Clinton E. Stockwell, director, Urban Church Resource Center, SCUPE

Previous articles have given some hints about the many different forms active Christian presence might take in city life. We have seen that the city is a multi-ethnic, multicolored phenomenon. To borrow a phrase from René Padilla's *The Contextualization of the Gospel*, one might say that it reflects the "many faceted wisdom of God." In "The Future—on Earth as It Is in Heaven," Tom Sine identifies some important historical images of the city in North America, and Samuel Wilson, in "The Field Is the World," points out that these historical images and feelings are often reflected in the church's approach to urban ministry today.

The purpose of this article is to point out some of the barriers to active Christian presence in local urban communities and then to suggest some helpful strategies for evangelization in the city. Evangelization can be defined somewhat broadly as the process by which the good news of the kingdom of God is told and lived out in the world. Evangelization here is not identified with any one evangelistic technique or method, but with creative strategies for bringing the Gospel as a whole to a particular local setting.

This approach is based on a number of theological perspectives: the Reformed doctrine of the importance and goodness of creation, even though it is alienated from God; Brueggemann's concept of the significance of "place," or shared commitments and experiences tied to a particular location over time; the Old Testament exhortation to Israel to seek the *shalom* or wholeness and well-being of its captor city Babylon (Jeremiah 29:7); and the Anabaptist teachings on purity and community in the church, without their tendency to see holiness or separation from the world in geographical terms. Evangelization is bringing the Gospel to individual urban neighborhoods, so that "the name of the city from that day will be *Yahweh, Shamah* [the Lord is there]" (Ezekiel 48:35).

BARRIERS TO NEIGHBORHOOD EVANGELIZATION

The following are some of the internal and external barriers to evangelization and effective neighborhood ministry that local urban churches might expect to encounter.

The first of these barriers is theological narrowness. This narrowness can

95

be intentional. Many church groups deliberately focus on one particular method of evangelism to the exclusion of all others. The result is almost always a gospel that is simplistic, reductionist, and inappropriate to community needs and circumstances. In addition, these techniques do little to prepare people to seek the renewal and *shalom* of their city (Jeremiah 29:7).

Theological narrowness may also take the form of preoccupations with single-issue concerns like inerrancy, dispensationalism, speaking in tongues, abortion, or denominational fidelity. Dogmatism tends to short-change our understanding of the many different cultures, theologies, classes, and lifestyles that coexist in the city. One example might be the church-growth movement, which appears to deliberately inhibit diversity for the sake of homogeneity. Like its counterpart, ecclesiastical imperialism, the church-growth movement seems to preclude a mutuality of cultures and the possibility of cross-cultural evangelism or shared celebration. Such thinking appears to fall short both biblically and sociologically, first by undercutting opportunities for *shalom*, peace, and reconciliation among different peoples, and second, by effectively ignoring the pluralistic reality of the city.

A second barrier to urban evangelization is racism and the fear of crime. Gibson Winter has called the present flight from the inner city to the suburbs and to the city periphery the "suburban captivity of the churches" in his book of the same name. Crime and the effects of racism are unquestionably multiplied among the poor, the homeless, and the unemployed in central cities; but, according to Luke, those are the very ones for whom the Gospel is intended (Luke 4:13-18). This raises some serious questions for the church about its lack of commitment to the poor and its growing identification with middle-class success, affluence, and upward mobility. The great white exodus to the suburbs after World War II all but drained the cities of skills and needed resources. The relatively few remaining urban commuter churches generally did not encourage strategic wholistic involvement in their parishes. The results have been transitional neighborhoods where the possibilities of *shalom* are greatly diminished.

A third barrier to evangelization is the individualistic spirit of modern Protestantism. Most Protestants see faith primarily in terms of personal response. As a group, they tend to be upwardly mobile, and are generally devoid of commitments to a particular neighborhood or parish, so that Protestants, more than Catholics, tend to move out of older neighborhoods as soon as it is economically feasible. This movement is often justified by a religious view of financial success as a reward for faithfulness. Many of these individuals are also reluctant to accept other persons who might be different in appearance or lifestyle. The white flight to the suburbs was primarily an escape from the perceived threat of blacks, Hispanics, and Asians. Under these circumstances, the gospel of reconciliation is thwarted before it even has a chance to operate.

A fourth barrier to evangelization is a persistent preoccupation with costly programs and structures that replaces investment in the spiritual and physical needs of the community. Often the success of a church is measured by the dimensions of its sanctuary, the size of its congregation, or the number of programs run by its professional staff, rather than by its concern for the neighborhood.

The Gospel is primarily concerned about the welfare of the hungry, the thirsty, the homeless, the sick, and the imprisoned. Programs not addressed to the real needs of people seem antithetical to the kingdom of God.

A fifth barrier is diminishing resources in the urban church, not only because of the exodus of the white church but also because of denominational strategies directed at planting new churches rather than maintaining old ones. The ladder of success often points urban pastors outward to newer, larger churches. As a result, inner-city clergy frequently find themselves alienated from their professional peers and undersupplied by denominational aid. This lack of emotional and financial support often results in burnout and discouragement.

Even though inner-city ministry is unquestionably more demanding than other kinds of pastorates, untrained and underqualified ministers are continually appointed to these smaller urban congregations, while more experienced urban pastors generally graduate to larger churches with greater emotional and financial health. The result is a case of diminishing returns for the urban church, a classic "Catch-22" in which urban churches do not grow and improve because the more experienced clergy constantly move on to easier situations.

A sixth barrier to evangelization is traditions and worship styles that are no longer relevant, adaptable, or expressive of newer community populations. It is important that existing traditions and histories be celebrated and lifted up, but not at the expense of multi-ethnic worship patterns that might attract neighborhood newcomers. Churches risk becoming irrelevant when they fail to allow mutuality, the chance for each group to hear its own voice and its own sound in the life of the church.

A seventh barrier to effective evangelization is the relative absence of lay participation in ministry. A more biblical understanding of ministry incorporates the whole people of God (the *Laos* of the New Testament, 1 Peter 2:9), using and developing their gifts, talents, and resources in the community. The layperson is usually the best point of contact with the community because he or she works and lives next to his or her neighbors, and shares many of the same burdens. If the church is an effective caring community, the whole church will tend to be involved in some form of evangelization. However, the wide range of spiritual gifts described in the New Testament points out that not everyone is expected to do the same thing. Personalities, cultures, and community identities and needs all vary a great deal. Sensitive evangelization attempts to match the gifts and resources present in the congregation with critical needs in the community. This approach results in strategies of evangelization that are contextualized, or adapted and suited to the neighborhood in its particular time and setting. From this perspective evangelization is seen more as a process of communal incarnation and less as a fixed program.

A final barrier to evangelization is a negative image of, or lack of vision for the urban neighborhood. The first doctrine of the Bible affirms the goodness and significance of creation, and of humanity's premier place in it. Being made in the image of God suggests that women and men have the potential to creatively reshape the world. Later in the Old Testament, God specifically directs the Babylonian exiles to seek the welfare or *shalom* of that city (Jeremiah 29:7). Surely this same message applies to the church in Chicago, New Orleans, Bangkok, and Mexico City.

BRIDGES TO
ACTIVE CHRISTIAN PRESENCE IN THE WORLD

In addition to seeing new possibilities for urban neighborhoods, and to adopting a more biblical, more wholistic understanding of the nature of evangelization, many bridges or paths to effective urban ministry may be listed.

One of these is the bridge of sensitivity and awareness to specific community needs. Programs and strategies are often ineffective when they are developed from an outsider's point of view. A sensitive and relevant church will attempt to understand community needs and problems as expressed by the people who live there.

A second bridge is the creation of cooperative networks with other churches and agencies in the area. Competition by churches is almost always unhealthy for the neighborhood as a whole. If one church has a food pantry, another could sponsor a day-care center for single and/or working parents. Nor is there any need for churches to duplicate the services of secular agencies. On the contrary, church support of these agencies could do much to connect communities with existing resources. One way the church will earn its right to be heard is by demonstrating its concern for neighborhood issues, including livable streets. Third World missionaries have learned that effective urban mission "must be socially involved if it is to be relevant. It cannot be simply a middle-class movement based on personal faith" (Jijot, 1980: 25).

A third bridge is having a repertoire of creative, effective urban ministry models, such as those of Jubilee Housing in Washington, D.C.; the Voice of Calvary in Jackson, Mississippi; or the LaSalle Street Church in Chicago, Illinois. Besides these evangelical examples, there is also renewal among mainline urban churches: the Church of the Holy Innocents in Hoboken, New Jersey; the Church of the Savior in Washington, D.C.; and the Church of the Redeemer in Houston, Texas. Other examples could be cited, of course, and many more such ministries are needed. Openness and dialogue between existing churches and emerging ministries can result in fellowship, exchange of ideas, and increased ministry effectiveness for all.

A fourth bridge is competent leadership, specifically trained for urban ministry. This background might include conflict management skills, community organizing skills, and networking skills, as well as practical skills in home weatherization and home improvement. Information about and access to existing urban resources would help pastors to avoid a one-person approach to ministry. This kind of training would match the real needs of the community, and provide the urban pastor with experience and task expertise that are at least as important as formal theological education. Continuing education, skills development, and on-the-job training are also important for urban clergy. New pastors might find it helpful to be apprenticed and evaluated for a time by more experienced supervising urban pastors.

Because laypersons, too, are seeking more opportunities for skills development, the church's educational task will be increasingly focused on "Equipping the saints for the work of service" (Ephesians 4:12). The catalog of spiritual gifts in Scripture suggests that this work of service will also be varied and relevant to needs both within and outside the church.

A fifth bridge is meaningful and effective educational methods that are person-centered and that encourage analytical thinking and the development of problem solving skills. Community involvement by the local church is usually best preceded by some form of analysis of the issues facing the neighborhood, and by exposure to various ministry options that might be adopted and adapted to the local context.

Experience-oriented education is also fruitful. In the course, "Conceptions of a City," SCUPE interns spend two weeks talking to people who live in the city and who reflect a number of individual perspectives and interests. Such an approach exposes students to the needs, issues, and life experiences of a variety of city dwellers from a resident's point of view.

A wide variety of educational methods are available to seminaries and to individual churches. Suggestions include personal interviews with community residents, neighborhood visits, case studies, dramatizations, simulation games, and cross-cultural experiences, as well as more traditional approaches such as lectures, sermons, and discussion groups.

A sixth bridge is increased cross-cultural awareness and greater openness to other races and ethnic groups. Fear and rejection of those who are different is often nothing more than fear and rejection of the unknown. Contact with other races and cultures can be perceived as potentially enriching, as well as threatening, though it will almost certainly challenge stereotypes. In cross-cultural churches, there are opportunities to listen to other cultures, and to affirm each one's place in the kingdom. A church that is open and secure in its own Christian identity is able to encourage the creative expression of constituent cultures in its life and liturgy. If the Gospel burns through racial and cultural barriers, then the presence of many nationalities in the neighborhood church reflects a microcosm of the kingdom.

A seventh bridge is the resource of underused church buildings that could be more available to the community and to its activities. If the community were encouraged to come into the church just as the church goes into the world, it might do much to promote mutual openness and understanding. The potential for evangelization and church growth are obvious. One example is the First Baptist Church of Evanston, Illinois, where the pastor moderated a forum for the local unemployed. According to the *American Baptist*, this church grew because of his demonstration of integrity and concern for the neighborhood (Jennings, 1982:22-24).

An eighth bridge is the potential for church leadership in the community. Anthony Campolo describes some practical steps for exercising this kind of leadership, as well as the tremendous potential of this style. According to Campolo, most local political and community groups attract an extremely small following. He suggests that if a half-dozen members of a small church would express enough sincere interest in their community to attend these meetings *quietly* and faithfully for just one year, their voices would be heard, and chances are they would be in leadership positions by the second year. He cautions that this approach be carried out tactfully, respectfully, and nonobtrusively, so that nonbelievers are not alienated from the church.

Church participants in the Discovery Program, a consulting project co-sponsored by SCUPE and ten Chicago Evangelical Covenant churches, have been surprised at the openness and cooperation of local community groups, schools, real estate agencies, and others in response to their in-quiries. The agencies visited were equally happy and surprised that churches were concerned about their neighborhoods. Most community groups want a better quality of life for their neighborhoods. While some community systems may be inefficient, unjust, and discriminatory, others share the same concerns as the Old Testament prophets for justice, compassion, and *shalom*.

Cooperation with existing agencies and government services is therefore recommended where possible. There is no need for the church to duplicate what others are already doing. Resources in the city are too scarce for that. However, the church can act responsibly by challenging existing social systems to insure a greater likelihood that city services are provided efficiently, justly, and humanely in all neighborhoods. This prophetic voice complements an active presence in the community.

A ninth bridge is support for financially strained urban churches. Possible funding sources include denominations, personal contributions, suburban-urban church networks, and wage and stipendiary funds for urban pastors. As one urban pastor said of suburban dwellers, "They moved to the suburbs because they wanted good schools, less crime, and more opportunities. . . we want that for our city neighborhoods as well."

A tenth bridge is long-term commitments both to individual urban ministries and to the city per se. An urban pastor in New Orleans once said that the first two years of his pastorate he was a liability to his church and its neighborhood. Short-term commitments do not allow time to adjust to a new environment or to get to know a community. Extended placements allow the new pastor to establish roots, and to build the networks and create the personal and community relationships that are the basis of effective evangelization.

Cities today are increasing both in size and in number. More needy persons are concentrated in the world's larger cities than ever before. The church's continued concern for these urban poor is a test of the integrity of its message. Jesus himself visited all the towns and cities of ancient Palestine, and Paul established missionary outposts in the urban centers of his time.

One sign of active Christian concern for the city is the presence of believers who are willing to live in urban neighborhoods themselves, rather than just supporting urban missions from a distance. According to Dr. Philip Amerson, a SCUPE adjunct faculty, "It's easier to talk favorably *about* the poor than to be *with* them" (Amerson, 1979:27). The value of Christians as role models, friends, resources, and facilitators in urban neighborhoods can hardly be overstated. A tangible, visible Christian community is a sign of the kingdom of God, and a physical demonstration that the Gospel is meaningful, relevant, and true.

An eleventh bridge or series of bridges is the deployment of a variety of evangelistic strategies and methods. Evangelization in the city requires creative thought, exploration, and experimentation because different peoples and cultures respond in different ways. Strategies that are effective in the suburbs may not be appropriate in the inner city, and programs that worked in other times or places may not be relevant today. In particular, tent revivals and mass evangelistic meetings often fall short because evangelists are not rooted in the neighborhood. Paul himself spent three years in Ephesus, and a year and a half in Corinth. Most urban revivalism today has a tendency to leave neighborhoods empty when the professional evangelist leaves. Training individual believers to assume leadership in community evangelization would probably have more enduring results. The church would do well to remember that Jesus did not have a consistent or stereotyped approach to evangelism. Each incident or story had its own setting and drew its own unique response.

A twelfth bridge is an all-inclusive Christian strategy for the city as a whole. Evangelization on this scale would require cooperation, organization, and networking strategies. The Christian church in the city now appears small, limited, and fragmented. The whole church working together across denominational lines could pool its scarce resources, and this cooperation would also confirm the integrity of its witness. Programs might begin in individual neighborhood churches and then expand as overall strategies are developed that allow other churches to share responsibilities throughout the city.

A final bridge is continuing education in cross-cultural communications and expanded cross-cultural contacts for both urban clergy and laypersons. Successful urban evangelization requires cooperation with and feedback from urban minority and ethnic leaders. The task of bringing the Gospel to pluralistic neighborhoods is too large and too complex not to make use of any and all available resources. It is also too important to be done by white strategists in isolation from minority leadership.

TOWARDS NEIGHBORHOOD EVANGELIZATION

Evangelization has been defined as the process by which the good news of the kingdom of God becomes manifest in a particular community in a tangible way. This final section will suggest some of the steps urban pastors might take to prepare a neighborhood evangelization strategy.

The first priority is to get to know the neighborhood and to discover its needs. Our first suggestion is the technique known as neighborhood mapping, using the traditional boundaries of the neighborhood. Official neighborhood maps can usually be obtained from the mayor's office of planning and development, the department of streets, real estate offices, school districts, fire and police stations, and so forth. The idea is to walk through the neighborhood and note on the map locations of agencies, institutions, places of employment, stores, parks, and public places; to note the conditions of housing, parks, streets, and institutions; and to write down impressions about the tour and about places that might merit a second visit.

The next step would be to set up appointments with local agencies, businesses, political leaders, police officers, and any others who might logically have information on local trends, perceived issues and actual neighborhood needs. These leaders may also be able to identify other persons to contact. Visiting social service and advocate groups is another way to gain insights about the neighborhood. It is also important to interview some community residents to determine their own understanding of neighborhood issues, needs, and problems. If someone is addressing these issues and needs, it is helpful to visit these individuals or agencies and observe what is actually being done. Another useful piece of information is to find out who the leading families are, to identify the influential people and decision-makers in the community, and to discover what or who influences these individuals when they make their decisions. Local bazaars, civic functions, and neighborhood meetings offer important opportunities for creating new friendships and networks along the way and also for building a community data base. It is especially important to note where residents gather at night. In many cities, bars or pubs were centers of local social and political activity and remnants of this tradition exist even today.

Visiting pastors of other community churches is a good way to get to know them, and to find out about their perceptions of the neighborhood and about their own approach to minstry. New pastors can also introduce themselves and their own objectives. Interviewing persons in one's own church, especially the old storytellers, will help furnish a more complete picture of the character of the neighborhood, and will also enable pastors to get to know their own parishioners.

Good sources of hard data on the neighborhood are the mayor's office, local universities, and main branches of the public libraries, all of which should have current census data. With this information, a pastor can target some of the issues and need groups in the community. Information may also be obtained from the Department of Housing and Urban Development (HUD), specialized libraries, school boards, community organizations, real estate headquarters, social service agencies, hospitals, and police and fire departments. Local statistics on demography, age breakdown, crime rates, mobility, occupational status, percentage of owner-occupied housing units, and the number of single-parent households, as well as future city plans for the neighborhood are all important in understanding the community. To track down old and recent newspaper stories about the neighborhood, pastors can consult city historical societies or municipal libraries with neighborhood or area clippings files. With this kind of background and awareness, with a comprehensive data base, and with community support, a church is ready to think about becoming more visibly involved in its place of ministry.

Throughout this process, it is important to get to know the people in the neighborhood and in the congregation. This means finding out who they are, where they work, where they go for social services, and what their special needs are. Usually it is best to rely on direct conversation with the people themselves rather than on secondhand information.

Once hard data and personal impressions about the community have been gathered, needs can be matched with the agencies and resources that are presently available or that could potentially address those needs. If pastors do not become catalysts or movers in these problem areas, they can at least be information-brokers who point others to appropriate resources. It is also important to take congregational resources into account. The gifts, talents, and resources (including time) in the congregation all increase its potential for evangelization.

Another key step is to assess honestly one's own personal and church limitations. Given the pressing needs usually found in urban neighborhoods, it is all too easy to develop a Messianic complex, and to act as if things will not get done unless the pastor does them. All believers in the neighborhood are part of the larger body of Christ. Working together, each gives support to the other for effective evangelization.

Now that some grasp of community issues, needs, and available resources has been obtained, it is time to begin jotting down some goals, objectives, and strategies for church involvement. Ideally, goal-setting is done with, not for, the congregation. If the congregation is not involved at this stage, chances are it will lose interest or refuse to cooperate. Setting reasonable and attainable goals is difficult enough even when there are no appreciable obstacles. Inner-city ministry requires that all available resources be tapped from the beginning if goals are to have a good chance of succeeding. As the church begins to formulate its strategies it is also helpful for the pastor to reevaluate his or her own theological assumptions about ministry and about personal goals for involvement. If possible, the pastor should live in the community where the church is located. John M. Perkins and the Voice of Calvary staff speak of the "three R's of the quiet revolution: relocation, redistribution, and reconciliation" (Perkins, 1976; Perkins, 1982). Relocation may be likened to incarnation, that is, the church becomes part of the community just as "the Word became flesh and dwelt among us." Redistribution relates to the just dispersal of goods and services in poorer neighborhoods. Reconciliation is the process of breaking down barriers to wholeness or *shalom*.

It is also important that a church develop a caring community, a visible and meaningful fellowship. According to Emil Brunner, *"ekklesia* precedes evangelism" (Brunner, 1955:154-159). Biblically, evangelism grows out of the life of the church. It may well be that a church needs to discover its own identity before it can share that identity with the neighborhood and before any outside action is meaningful. If there is a sense of Christian community at church, then models of Christian family life, benevolence, and care will help the community to see and hear the Gospel even before any formal evangelistic outreach occurs. The news that churches bring to urban neighborhoods is good news, offering hope and direction. The bad news of judgment and rejection is already there, especially for the poor. It is the unjust systems, the rich and the powerful, who need judgment and challenge.

It is equally important both to consider programs that encourage the community to come into the church if it is not already there, and to encourage congregation participation in existing community organizations. New outreach ministries should probably not be undertaken unless needs are not otherwise addressed in the neighborhood, and then only if gifts, personnel, and resources are available to staff and support new programs adequately.

Neighborhood people will expect to see some of their own forms of expression in liturgy and worship. Dialogue with and openness to indigenous peoples, old and new, are signs of a high quality relationship between a church and its neighborhood. New converts and established believers alike can be challenged to growth, discipleship, and sensitivity to the needs of others both within and outside the fellowship.

Urban evangelization is an ongoing process that involves hard work and the struggle for creative growth. However, as urban churches begin to bear the burdens and joys of their own neighborhoods, they may also discover it to be revitalizing and even fun.

REFERENCES CITED

Amerson, Philip. 1979. Excess or Access: Bringing in the Least of These. *Sojourners*. July.

Brunner, Emil. 1955. Ecclesia and Evangelism. *Japan Christian Quarterly*. April.

Jennings, Ray. 1982. One Church's Response to the Unemployed. *The American Baptist*. November.

Jijot, P. 1980. The Power and the Conflict: Christ's Legacy in Asia. *Far Eastern Economic Review*. April.

Perkins, John A. 1976. *A Quiet Revolution*. Waco: Word.

———. 1982. *With Justice for All*. Ventura, California: Gospel Light.

SELECTED ANNOTATED BIBLIOGRAPHY

Berger, Alan S. *The City: Urban Communities and Their Problems.* Dubuque: William C. Brown, 1978.

A significant urban sociology text. Berger argues that cities are dynamic processes which effect the viability of human community in dense urban settlements.

Boerma, Conrad. *The Rich, the Poor and the Bible.* Philadelphia: Westminster, 1979.

Boerma notes how the word "poor" is used in the Bible; as an indication of unrighteousness, as an example of oppression, and as a spiritual virtue. The church community is the basis of solidarity in the New Testament, and the community exists to share its wealth with those who are economically poor.

Callow, Alexander B. ed., *American Urban History: An Interpretive Reader with Commentaries.* 3rd ed. New York: Oxford University Press, 1982.

This is a collection of essays isolating the main themes of the urban experience in the United States. Essays are on Winthrop's Boston, urban reform, industrialization, immigration, urban renewal, social conflict, and so forth.

Chudacoff, Howard P. *The Evolution of American Urban Society.* rev. ed. Englewood Cliffs, New Jersey: Prentice Hall, 1981.

A recently revised, highly readable, short work on the history and development of the U.S. city. Chudacoff focuses on the plight of the poor in U.S. urban history. Excellent bibliographies are listed at the end of each chapter.

Cox, Harvey. *The Secular City.* New York: Macmillan, 1966.

A classic theological essay on the meaning of the city. Cox celebrates secularism, and anticipates that the church will need to be more secular and human if it is to be relevant. He was partly right.

Davis, James H. and Woodie W. White. *Racial Transition in the Church.* Nashville: Abingdon, 1980.

These authors deal with the critical problem of churches in transitional communities. Chapters are on the dilemmas and patterns of racial transition, with a concluding chapter on strategies for churches facing changing neighborhoods.

Dudley, Carl S. *Making the Small Church Effective.* Nashville: Abingdon, 1980.

Carl Dudley is acutely sensitive to the needs of the small church in a changing urban neighborhood. Dr. Dudley believes that a church can be effective if a caring community is created as the church remembers its history, traditions, and its historic commitment to neighborhood places.

Ellison, Craig, ed. *The Urban Mission.* Grand Rapids: Eerdmans, 1974.

A unique collection of essays documenting the history, theologies, methods, and models of urban mission. A very helpful collection despite the fact that some of the models are no longer around.

Fischer, Claude S. *To Dwell Among Friends: Personal Networks in Town and City.* Chicago: University of Chicago, 1982.

Dr. Fischer is a noted sociologist, the author of *The Urban Experience.* He notes that urban life is *not* detrimental to health, community, ethnicity, or even religious faith. In fact urban life "supports rather than weakens" these experiences.

Frenchak, David J. and Sharrel Keyes, eds. *Metro-Ministry.* Elgin, Illinois: David C. Cook, 1980.

A very helpful collection of essays, derived from the 1978 Congress on Urban Ministry. Raymond Bakke's "Biblical Theology for the City;" Anthony Campolo's "Sociology of the Urban Church;" and Frenchak's "Urban Fatigue" are most timely.

Greenway, Roger S., ed. *Discipling the City.* Grand Rapids: Baker Book House, 1979.

A good collection of essays, subtitled "Theological Reflections on Urban Mission." The essayists represent mostly an evangelical Calvinist point of view. Particularly helpful is Harvie Conn's adaption of H. Richard Niebuhr's *Christ and Culture* stereotypes for mission today. Sidney Rooy's article on "Theological Education for Urban Mission" is excellent and worth the price of the book.

Hessel, Dieter. *Social Ministry*. Philadelphia: Westminster, 1982.

Hessel believes that the church's parish role is to develop a "whole ministry." A key chapter is "Renewal of Community Ministry" in which the author advocates concrete involvement in the areas of social service, community organization, and public policy formulation.

Jacobs, Jane. *The Death and Life of the Great American Cities*. New York: Random House-Vintage, 1961.

A classic critique of the "top-down" policies of the urban renewal epoch in recent U.S. history. The author holds that the life of the city is in the vitality of its neighborhoods.

Noyce, Gaylord. *Survival and Mission for the City Church*. Philadelphia: Westminster, 1975.

A very practical handbook. Noyce isolates biblical images for urban ministry, and proceeds to chapters on resources for the urban church, options for the downtown church, and the importance of a "Christian stance in the secular city."

O'Connor, Elizabeth. *Journey Inward, Journey Outward*. New York: Harper & Row, 1968.

O'Connor's many books document the internal struggles of a mainline church adapting to a changing neighborhood. The Church of the Savior in Washington, D.C. has since become a model of community, creativity, and innovative ministry commitment.

Palen, J. John. *The Urban World*. 2nd ed. New York: McGraw-Hill, 1981.

An excellent sociology text on world urbanization with up-to-date statistics, profiles, and projections of the impact of urbanization locally and globally.

Pasquariello, Ronald D., Donald Shriver, Jr., and Alan Geyer. *Redeeming the City*. New York: Pilgrim, 1982.

The authors argue persuasively that involvement in urban ministry necessarily involves one in challenging urban public policy with alternative suggestions.

Perkins, John M. *With Justice for All*. Ventura, California: Regal, 1982.

The founder of The Voice of Calvary Ministries in Jackson, Mississippi (and elsewhere), focuses in this book on the economic importance of community development and reconciliation through the church. In this book Perkins gives his three R's of the quiet revolution more concrete expression.

Ryan, William. *Blaming the Victim.* New York: Random House-Vintage, 1976.

Ryan is a psychologist and argues in this book that poor communities, especially minorities, are victims of oppressive social institutions rather than causes of their own plight. His initial discussion on how and why affluent persons "blame the victim" is upsetting, but true.

Sider, Ronald J., ed. *Evangelicals and Development: Toward a Theology of Social Change.* Philadelphia: Westminster, 1982.

The authors attempt to relate theology from an Anabaptist perspective to the need for community development among the poor, especially the poor of the Third World. The authors argue for a theology of social change.

Sine, Tom. *The Mustard Seed Conspiracy.* Waco, Texas: Word, 1982.

Dr. Sine is a "futurist" by profession. This book collects his thoughts on the nature of Christian community, lifestyle change, and anticipating tomorrow's future. The kingdom of God begins as an insignificant mustard seed, but has great potential for the developing and underdeveloped worlds.

Sowell, Thomas. *Ethnic America.* New York: Basic Books, 1981.

Sowell traces the histories of old and new ethnic groups in blacks, Asians, and Hispanics with excellent supporting statistical data on each ethnic group's present situation in the United States.

Tonna, Benjamin. *Gospel for the Cities.* Translated by William E. Jerman. Maryknoll, New York: Orbis, 1982.

The Italian Catholic author documents the fact of urbanization and the plight of the poor in Third World cities. Tonna argues for significant planning and an orderly response to urban needs with implications for the church's world-wide urban mission and evangelization.

Warren, Donald I. and Rachelle B. Warren. *The Neighborhood Organizer's Handbook.* South Bend, Indiana: University of Notre Dame, 1977.

The authors assist greatly in typifying and identifying types of neighborhoods. Particularly helpful for urban pastors are the chapters "The Bridging Role of the Neighborhood Activist" and "How to Diagnose a Neighborhood."

Webber, George W. *The Congregation in Mission.* Nashville: Abingdon, 1964.

This work is subtitled, "Emerging Structures of the Church in Urban Society." The author points out suggestions for the church's mission in response to growing urban problems and needs. Webber's books are of significant help for the urban congregation.

Winter, Gibson. *The Suburban Captivity of the Churches.* New York: Macmillan, 1962.

Winter argues that the white flight of the churches to the suburbs indicates a betrayal of the mission of the church. An active Christian presence in the city on the part of the church is redemptive for the city, and for the church.

Yoder, John Howard. *The Politics of Jesus.* Grand Rapids: Eerdmans, 1972.

An enduring Anabaptist theology for sociopolitical involvement based on a concrete and literal interpretation of the jubilary themes in Leviticus and in Jesus' "inaugural address" in Luke 4:13-18.

INDEX

111